WHAT PEOPLE ARE SAYING ABOUT

DEATH, THE LAST GOD

This is one of those invaluable books that after reading we discover has changed us forever. It is a brilliant contribution to a modern dialogue on the meaning of death. I will be recommending this book to anyone interested not only in death, but also in life.
Aleine Ridge, Interfaith Minister, Director of Spiral Holistic Therapy Centre

Anne Geraghty is an experienced therapist and group facilitator whose only son unexpectedly died. This book reveals a deeply personal journey and a new understanding of Living and Dying. It is a 21st century companion to Sogyal Rinpoche's classic *The Tibetan Book of Living and Dying*. It contains a wealth of ideas that I can already envisage using in my teaching and facilitation.
Dr Mike Fitter, Consultant Psychologist, Amida Buddhist

Anne Geraghty has written a book for our time. Having endured the unspeakably premature loss of her son, Anne courageously presents a personal documentary of a mother's grief and combines this with a vivid and multilayered inquiry. A scholar's mind, a mother's heart, and the grit that comes from honouring unconscious forces, all work together to bring us to an exhilarating and challenging edge within ourselves.
Barbara Brown, Creator of bodytao therapy and qi gong; Author of *Qi Gong: The Chinese Art of working with energy, Looking for Doris* and *Han Returns to Earth*.

Reading this book felt like standing on the edge of the Grand Canyon. I was awestruck and opened by the magnificent view. This book is a dance between grief and intelligent enquiry involving a fascinating, engaging, multicultural approach. It is a gift to humanity.

Jenny Suzumoto, MA in Counselling Psychology, Spiritual Director, Portland, Oregon, US

This passionate and deeply felt book travels through the underworld of extreme grief and emerges with real wisdom. Anne Geraghty respects the great spiritual traditions but also looks beyond them and offers a vivid, individual vision of the great mystery of death. I recommend this to all who are facing or thinking about death.

Lyn Webster Wilde, Author of *Becoming the Enchanter*

Death the Last God is unlike any other book on death. This really is a modern Book of the Dead. It is not an easy read because it confronts many of society's assumptions about death and challenges us to think for ourselves. Yet whatever we conclude about death after reading this, one thing is sure, we will never see death in the same light again. This is a book for our times.

Maggie La Tourelle, Author of *The Gift of Alzheimer's* and *Principles of Kinesiology*

This book creates a paradigm shift into a new way of thinking of death. Anne conveys complex ideas with humour and compassion, while her wisdom goes right into the heart of what it means to be alive and human.

Sandra Hailes, BA, PG Dip in Psychotherapy, MBACP, Bereavement Counsellor

The day my spiritual teacher Osho died, my daughter San Chi was born. So it was, simultaneously, 'Death of a Master, Birth of a Child'. The two together – certainly in me. Anne Geraghty took the hard way to realise that union, after the untimely death of her son, Tim. In this book she records her way out of this so-personal disaster, drawing on views from many times and places, to discover life and death are hand in hand – like Osho and San Chi – but too, in the very same person. Her Tim.

Michael Barnett, Cosmic Energy Master, Author of 40 books in English

Anne brings a depth and openness to her exploration of this challenging topic that go way beyond traditional religious and spiritual beliefs and even contemporary approaches. The result is a fresh and illuminating conversation that touches the soul and asks us to expand our idea of what is possible amidst the great mystery of death... and life.

Amoda Maa Jeevan, Spiritual Teacher and Author of *Change Your Life, Change Your World* and *How to Find God in Everything*

In this book Anne weaves together a tapestry that brings together psychotherapeutic knowledge, many wisdom traditions and Western science with the raw very human experience of death. The result is both a unique contribution to our understanding and a comforting embrace of death's possibilities. It's a book to feed every part of our being – from the depths of our belly and heart to our mind and our soul.

Jan Day, Conscious Relationships & Living Tantra Workshops & Coaching

Death,
the Last God

A Modern Book of the Dead

Death,
the Last God

A Modern Book of the Dead

Anne Geraghty

BOOKS

Winchester, UK
Washington, USA

First published by O-Books, 2014
O-Books is an imprint of John Hunt Publishing Ltd., Laurel House, Station Approach,
Alresford, Hants, SO24 9JH, UK
office1@jhpbooks.net
www.johnhuntpublishing.com

For distributor details and how to order please visit the 'Ordering' section on our website.

ISBN: 978 1 78279 709 8

A CIP catalogue record for this book is available from the British Library.

Design: Stuart Davies

Printed and bound by CPI Group (UK) Ltd, Croydon, CR0 4YY

We operate a distinctive and ethical publishing philosophy in all
areas of our business, from our global network of authors to
production and worldwide distribution.

CONTENTS

For Tim

Introduction

God announced that he would answer any question.
A young man rushed forward. 'What happens when we die?'
God killed him.

What happens when we die? Do we have one and only one life or are we reincarnated thousands of times? Does our spirit live on in paradise or only in the hearts and minds of those who loved us? Do our souls exist forever in another dimension or is death an absolute ending and we no longer exist?

We might try to work out what belief or idea about death is the right one, what is the 'truth', but there can be no objective answers to such questions because what is being addressed is a person not an event. Not only that; death, like life, has many dimensions. Some of the dimensions of death belong to our human world, aspects of the continual evolution of life on Earth. Other dimensions belong to the cosmos in a different way, elements of a mystery so vast we can never comprehend it. Reality is always greater than our ideas about it anyway. And whatever may be our beliefs about death, we will have direct experience of it one day.

Yet even though death is the one certainty in life, we tend not to think much about it. We focus more on creating a home, raising our families, making a living and enjoying ourselves than we do on the inevitability of our death. Naturally. We hardly want to ponder that this life will end while in the middle of making it. Yet sometimes we are brought face to face with death in a way that cannot be avoided.

My son, Tim, died suddenly at the age of thirty-four. After years of hard partying he had been off alcohol and drugs for six months because he and his wife were planning a family. That night, as he had done at many parties before, he drank and took a cocktail of drugs, but this time his tolerance was gone. He went to sleep and never woke up.

Tim was my only child; his death became a journey into death for me too. Yet even in the unspeakable pain of my grief I found dimensions of our relationship continued to unfold. Death is an absolute ending; it also holds a mysterious continuity.

During the first year of Tim's death, I experienced many inexplicable phenomena and had a series of vivid dreams in which my relationship with Tim continued, as I now know it always will. Not only because we loved each other deeply and that love is forever, but because I discovered there are as many realities and dimensions to death as there are to life, and many of the energies of life and death are eternal. Life on Earth creates realities and energies that do not simply disappear when we die; on the contrary, these become part of the fabric of existence. And although the death of someone we love is an inconsolable loss because that person is gone forever, there are discoveries in death that can nourish and sustain us in a different way.

My experiences of Tim's death did not conform to anything I had heard or read about death before. And anyway I could not accept unquestioningly the descriptions of life after death given by various religions. I therefore had to find my own way through the labyrinth. This book is my attempt to share some of what I learned.

Death, the Last God explores not only the many dimensions of death but also how different aspects of our human psyche describe and experience death differently. It examines various psycho-spiritual and cultural maps of what happens when we die to develop a modern understanding of death. And it explains how the language of Myth, which is about human truth and meaning, and Logos, which is concerned with empirical facts, use different languages to speak of the same event. We need this diversity.

In our modern world we have become complex individuals, and different parts of us die differently. The modern self contains a multitude of energies, sub-personalities, selves and archetypes, and when we experience a death each of these aspects will use a different language and myth to give that death its significance and meaning. Some aspects might speak of death as a return home, others of death as a profound goodbye to literally all that matters, the material world. For some aspects death is a transformation, for others, annihilation. Some aspects may remain in life as memories or legacies; others may dissolve into a mystery beyond our comprehension. Just as we weave our unique experiences into a narrative of life, we each find the narrative or myth that gives meaning to our death. And that narrative is likely to include contradictory and apparently opposing ideas because of the complexity of our modern psyche. When Tim died I shattered into a multitude of pieces, and each fragment experienced and described his death differently.

Some parts spoke of myths, memories and introjections, others of God, spirits and angels, others of energy fields, black holes and dark flow. I explored Christian, Pagan and Tibetan Buddhist ideas of death. I researched Near Death Experiences. I read astrophysics and linguistic philosophy. I had a series of vivid dreams unlike my usual dreaming. I went to an Ayahuasca ceremony with a shaman. A medium channelled information for me from the Spirit World. I reached out in all directions for anything that might explain what was happening to me in my grief. I was seeking answers to a multitude of questions, but most of all I was looking for Tim. Like Demeter, I searched everywhere for the child I had lost. It was a long time before I realised that what I was seeking would be found within myself.

Before Tim's death I had never thought much about death at all. What mattered was life here, not a fantasy afterlife with white lights, smiling bodhisattvas, angels on harps or thousands of virgins, depending on the brochure one read. I had the vague notion that when we die we dissolve back into existence, God, the light, stardust, I didn't mind what word was used, in much the same way our bodies dissolve back into dust. I believed that if we have truly lived life, and not just survived it, we bequeath whatever legacy we have created back into life as we leave. If asked I might have said that whatever we have been willing to die for will live on past our death. If we have been willing to die for peace, that is our legacy. If we have been willing to die for truth then that is what we leave behind. And if we have been willing to die for nothing, then that is our legacy – nothing. But death taught me many things – about our humanity as well as our spirit, about life as well as death.

I began to sense we do not leave our legacy behind at all; we become it. And in this is the mysterious renewal of life, through death, into more life. I discovered that death is not an event in the future with no relevance to us until it happens; life and death are inextricably interconnected and the reality of death permeates every moment. And I found that although death is a terrible and inconsolable loss, it is also a profound and inexplicable liberation.

When Tim had been dead three months Martin, my husband and Tim's stepfather, Jo, Tim's widow, and I went to Samye Ling, a Tibetan Buddhist monastery in Scotland. We were hoping to find spiritual direction and nourishment to ease the pain of our grief. While we were in the temple meditating Jo and Martin received clear messages. Jo was to take up her painting again and Martin was to meditate regularly. But there was no message for me.

I wandered into the Peace Garden thinking of course I would hear nothing – what kind of wisdom could reach a mother who had failed even to keep her son alive? I sat on a bench, bent over in despair. A voice spoke clearly and authoritatively: 'You must write a modern book of the dead.' I sat up in surprise and looked around, but there was no one there. I was probably inventing fantasy voices to distract myself from the awful finality of Tim's death. I was incapable of writing anything anyway, let alone about a massive subject like death. I was so lost in grief I spent most of my time inarticulately staring into a blank wall of inconsolable loss and weeping. But I did begin to write down my dreams, my strange experiences and the thoughts about death that arose from them. Not for a book, I told myself, just for me.

In the aftermath of Tim's death, on my quest to find out what had happened to Tim, where he had gone, who or what he had become, I consulted mediums, meditated, practised tuning in on realities beyond the mind, read books on life beyond death, channelling, astral travelling, anything that might give me clues as to what had happened to Tim. Once I went to a Spiritualist meeting.

About twenty of us sat on stackable chairs in a small community hall with Cyril. He asked one woman if she had been hoovering earlier. The woman sat up. 'Yes,' she said. 'And did your hoover break and did you swear at it?' 'Yes, I did,' she said. 'Someone is here – Susan, Suzie?' 'Susan, yes, my aunt!' she exclaimed. 'Well Susan says she saw you and wants you to know that she did not mind you swearing at all.' 'Oh thank you!' said the woman smiling. Cyril moved on to tell another that her father was very pleased with her recent success. Had she had a recent success? Yes she had just won £100 on a scratchcard. She sat back, her eyes shining. Her father had not gone completely; he was still with her.

One by one people heard from dead relatives, comforted to know their loved ones were still with them and cared about their knee operation, their new job, the death of their cat or whatever. Cyril was clearly a gifted man and gave everyone a message of some kind from beyond the grave. But there was none for me.

He asked me to stay behind. 'I want to speak to you privately,' he said. 'I have a different kind of message for you.' He closed his eyes. I waited. He told me: 'You have a silver box and in it are uncut diamonds that you must polish.' He opened his eyes and stared at me intently. 'You must do this, I am to tell you this is important,' he said.

This was rubbish. I do not have a silver box. Neither do I own any rough diamonds.

Cyril closed his eyes again and began to talk about my family. He gave me a message from my dead mother. 'Mary, Moira?' he asked. Her name was Myra. Maybe this was not complete rubbish after all. Still no message from Tim though. But Cyril had not finished. 'There's a young man here.' He opened his eyes. 'But you are far more connected with him than I could ever be. You don't need me. You two can communicate with each other with no problem. And there is something you have to do together.'

Well, I had been hoping for a connection with Tim, had wanted to find him again, not just in my dreams, as a memory, or in the feelings within my own heart; I had wanted some kind of proof. But here I was being told I was already connected, I already had what I was seeking. This was guidance of a kind, I suppose, even if not what I wanted. I thanked Cyril and drove home.

Many months later, I remembered what Cyril had said about my silver box and the uncut diamonds that needed polishing. A thought struck me – my MacBook is silver. Could he have been referring to my strange experiences since Tim's death, the vivid dreams and strange experiences that I had been writing down? Were these the rough diamonds I must polish? Maybe I could write a book on death after all. Maybe my experiences could be useful for others. This book did not have to have the answers as, of course, no such a book could be written. How could it? Only a dead person could write one. But dead men don't write, jump, wear plaid or do anything. I began to write about death, the ultimate journey into the unknown.

In this book, some chapters explore ideas and myths from other cultures, others wander into the realm of speculation, others describe my personal experience; as a consequence, frequently I have had to use metaphor to facilitate communication. This is not, therefore, a book of facts or knowledge; it is more an invitation to approach death differently. It is a contribution towards a dialogue about death because, both individually and collectively, we need such a dialogue. We need a modern narrative of death, which does not merely turn to mediaeval myths or ancient Eastern culture for answers but is rooted in our current understandings of human nature and the workings of the universe, because a conversation about death that embraces contemporary understandings of life will uncover new dimensions to the meaning of death and what happens when we die. Such understandings can then give us the ultimate freedom – to live one's own unique life and die one's own unique death. And then we can answer the question 'what is death?' Our life is our answer.

1

The Dark Side of the Moon

Death comes and shouts with no mouth, with no tongue, with no throat.
Pablo Neruda

The Hubble telescope transformed Astronomy when, instead of focusing on various celestial objects, it simply stared into what appeared to be empty space. Gradually faint light from nebulae and galaxies millions of light years away was detected, and events just moments after the Big Bang were seen. By gazing into an empty darkness, the story of the universe was revealed. When we gaze into the vast darkness of death, another great story is revealed. But seeing requires light – how does one look into complete darkness?

Creatures who live in the perpetual night of Deep Ocean, where no light reaches, create their own light. To see into the dark night of death we also have to create our own light. The very looking creates that light. So let us begin our exploration of death by looking right into the dark emptiness and losses of death.

Death is the end of the life of our body. Death is a night so dark it is the blackest black of having no eyes that will ever see again, the most silent silence of having no ears that will ever hear again, the emptiest void of having no mind that will ever think again. In all directions everything is gone. As Philip Larkin wrote: 'Only one ship is seeking us, a black-sailed unfamiliar, towing at her back a huge and birdless silence. In her wake no waters breed or break.'

When we die we all lose our ground, our body, our location in time and space, we no longer have our five senses, we do not

8

inhabit the material world, our animal instincts and drives are gone, we no longer struggle to survive nor fear death, and whatever our race, creed or nationality while alive, when we die we join the great community of the dead. We may each build our 'ship of death' differently but we all travel in her into the darkness of death.

Some of our beliefs of the afterlife are consoling ideas to escape the absolute finality of death. We might read Canon Scott-Holland's poem: 'Death is nothing at all, I have only slipped away into the next room… One brief moment and all will be as it was before.' This may bring comfort in the midst of desperate grief but if we always try to console the inconsolable we belittle both death and life.

Facing the inconsolability of loss through death is so profoundly painful we often do need comforting words to help us through our loss, but this does not help our understanding of what is death. Death is real and death is absolute. When we die we lose everything that matters to us, literally the material world. However many other aspects unfold when one dies, death, in part, involves a dark flight down into oblivion. If we do not honour the power and might of death, Death will never allow us into its magnificence. As Meister Eckhart, the 12th century mystic, wrote: 'The kingdom of God is for none but the thoroughly dead.'

Until we face the dreadful totality of death, our fear is likely to prevent an exploration of death with an open mind because inevitably we will turn to comforting fantasies to protect ourselves from the awful power of death to end a life. We might imagine that somehow we do not really die, we are transformed and everything is much the same as before, only better. But this is not the reality of death. When I die, Anne will be no more. When you die, the 'me' that you call yourself will be no more. As Albert Camus wrote: 'In order to exist just once in the world, it is necessary never again to exist.' And in this lies the awe-ful reality of death. The living body is gone forever. The unique individual self, inextricably linked to the body that dies, also can never exist again. And this utter finality breaks our hearts. It is therefore natural to try and find consolation where we can – but we diminish life when we diminish death.

And yet maybe there is more to this story.

When each of us dies, our essential qualities, our energetic presence, our vibrational being, our legacy, however we might describe our soul or spirit, might continue formlessly for some time after we have died. Anne may be gone as an entity with substance and shape but, like the sound of a bell may resound as a vibration long after it has been struck, and even long after we can no longer hear it, an anne-ness might continue in another way. But before we can explore what might happen to our consciousness, our love, and the essential qualities of our unique is-ness after death, first we must face our mortality. Because only when our sight is not blurred by fear and false hope can we see clearly whether death is the end or not.

My first night back home after the funeral, twelve days after Tim had died, I had a vivid dream.

I am in the large basement of a building with low ceilings surrounded by piles of old furniture, though I cannot see clearly as there is barely any light. Martin is with me. Suddenly there is a loud single knock on the door and a man dressed in black leather, motor-bike gear with black goggles and a tight black helmet, bursts through the door, followed by a tall thin man dressed in grey. The thin man turns to Martin who is a little away to my left but I cannot see what is happening there because the man in black leather comes straight over to me and sticks his face right into mine. It becomes the face of a grinning demon so full of unadulterated evil I am terrified. In a flash he grabs my shoulders and knocks me off my feet. He has tight hold of me, driving me backwards, my feet off the ground, as if my shoulders are the handlebars of a motorbike. We fly at terrific speed through the basement, his face pushed against mine in a maniacal grimace of pure evil. I have never been so terrified in my life.

The force and speed of what is happening is so intense, I cannot fight it, and there is nothing I can do but surrender. We fly hard and fast swerving between the pillars and the furniture. I am convinced at any moment my head will smash into something and, as we are going so fast, this will split my head open and I will die. I am absolutely petrified with fear. Suddenly I realise, the only power this demon has over me is in the terror he has created; he can do nothing directly. There is nothing to be afraid of, except my fear. The dream ends as abruptly as it began.

I puzzled over the dream. Suddenly I understood it. The evil demon was Tim's death.

Tim's death arrived in my life with a loud single knock on our front door by a policewoman in the night to tell us he was dead. Tim's death then rushed in and knocked me off my feet, terrifying me more than anything in my life had terrified me before. The fierce reality of death smacked into me and stared me in the face, appearing so overpoweringly evil that I had no choice but to surrender to it completely. The evil in this demon appeared to me to be the worst possible evil I could ever encounter, just as Tim's death was the worst possible thing I could envisage happening. Yet the demon of death has power over me only to the extent I am afraid of it. As Publilius Syrus wrote thousands of years ago, 'The fear of death is more to be dreaded than death itself.'

I also realised that I was no longer afraid of death. When the worst has happened what is there left to fear? This enabled me to look directly into death in a way I had not been able to before.

I had always thought that our spirit lived on, not in some mythical afterlife, but in life. We live on in the hearts of those who loved us, in the memories of people we knew, in our children, in a garden we designed, in a recipe we invented, in a song we wrote... Yet when Tim died I experienced inexplicable phenomena and a series of extraordinarily vivid dreams in which Tim and I explored death together. These forced me to question my beliefs about death. Do we live on in any other way? Is there some entity or being that lives on as a spirit? Or are these merely fairy tales to console the inconsolable?

The first day of Tim's death I could hardly move; movement reminded me that I was alive and Tim was dead. I lay on the sofa and stared into a dreadful void. At about 2 pm I felt a strange puzzlement in the air, moving around the room on the edge of my perception. Suddenly I sensed it was Tim. I did not hear words but it was as if he was asking me what was going on. 'Am I trapped in a nightmare, a fever or in a strange drug trip? Is this some kind of weird computer game, a virtual reality that I cannot escape? What is happening?' His confusion swirled around the room.

I felt a compulsion to speak aloud.

'Yesterday you were alive, and in the night, you died.'

I had no idea why I said this; I simply had to say it. I spoke slowly and clearly, stating it as a simple fact with no emotion. I repeated it six times.

The room became still. I sensed that Tim had heard me and now knew he was dead. A great silence fell – the silence of death.

Many spiritual and religious traditions say that frequently spirits of dead people need to be told they are dead. Shamans from as far apart as Siberia and South America speak of the spirits of dead people who hang around the living and must be told they are dead and ordered to leave. Taoist and Confucian traditions talk of 'hungry ghosts' who are too attached to the material plane or too full of vengeance for enemies still alive to acknowledge they are dead. In Tibet, they say that not only do people need to be told they have died, but as their mind deteriorates, they tend to forget and so often need to be told many times before they finally realise they have died. Christian exorcisms too have been not only of demons but also of the souls of people that have taken up residence within a living person because they do not know they are dead. Spirits of the dead still attached to this world are seen as trapped in a kind of prison where they need spirit-guides, angels, shamans, dead ancestors, religious figures and saints of all sorts to help them over the threshold into another realm. And not only spiritual types.

Air Chief Marshal Dowding was the commander of RAF Flight Command during the Battle of Britain in WW2. He described how during a mission he would sit quietly with his pipe and wait because frequently the souls of aircrew, shot down in fights with the Luftwaffe, would come to him to ask him in confusion what had happened; they did not know they had died. He said it was his duty to inform them that they had made the greatest sacrifice and given their lives for their country. He explained that they trusted him and would therefore listen when he told them they were dead.

Martin asked me why I had spoken as I had. I told him about Tim's puzzlement but could not explain why I spoke so slowly and repetitively. I simply knew I had to speak clearly as if to someone who did not understand English well and needed the words to be simple. Later I came to realise that when life leaves a body, and the body grows cold and dead, then the human cognitive mind is also gone. The neurones in the brain are no longer firing and the neural pathways that permit thought have ceased to operate. So when Tim's brain stopped functioning, his thinking processes inevitably faded very soon afterwards. Perhaps this is why I spoke as one would to a young child, who may be alert, feeling and conscious, but not intellectually sophisticated or thinking logically. An aspect of Tim was present, but his mind was fading.

It became another loss in a series of losses when I realised that Tim's brilliant mind and his wonderful way with words had absolutely and completely gone forever. But this was later, when I had also learned that our human mind with its capacity to think and speak is only part of our human intelligence. Perhaps there is a kindness in nature that allows us to absorb piece by piece the many losses that follow a sudden death. All at once and maybe it would kill us too. I was able to understand the absolute finality of death to the same degree I experienced a continuity of a different kind. And this process took me gradually, step by step, into a different understanding of death, in which death, like the dark emptiness of deep space, is more than the void it appears to be when we first look at it.

What is it that remains when the body has died? What part of the dead person are we communicating with when we tell them they have died? Perhaps it is the last remaining vestiges of a person's consciousness; after all, physiological death is not a singular event, different parts of the body die at different rates. Fingernails and hair can grow after death. The brain may show no electrical activity well before the liver ceases to function. Evidence from beheadings reveal that mouths and eyes can move for up to 30 seconds after the head is severed and the body can kick for even longer. Perhaps the consciousness of a person also takes a while to fade. Or maybe the experience of speaking to the spirit of a person is a form of our ongoing relationship with the one who has died. After all, when a person we love dies, the love does not disappear; it finds new forms in which to express itself.

Diverse cultures and religions claim there is a soul or spirit with a unique identity that lives on beyond the grave, but is this just a projection of our human longing for transcendence to escape the awful finality of death? Or does something of the unique person continue to exist beyond death, perhaps in the energy fields of reality even if no longer in the material realms, maybe as a vibration, a trace, a fragment of an existential hologram? Perhaps the dead make up the dark matter that is invisible yet, according to physicists, makes up 83% of the known universe, and without which existence would fall in on itself and cease. Or is death beyond all description and analysis, and forever a mystery that can be spoken about only in metaphor?

When exploring the unknown we are forced to use familiar language to communicate, yet common language has evolved to deal with the material world in time and space, not energies that transcend this. Many misunderstandings arise when we speak the same language but use it differently. Ludwig Wittgenstein wrote, 'The limits of my language is the limit of my world.' Perhaps we need a new language to speak of the mysteries of death. Either that or we understand the relativity of all language and recognise that whether we use the language of black holes or hell, archetypes or angels, memes or souls, the important thing is not the description of our experience so much as the meaning we give it.

Hotei was a monk who lived in the 10th century in China. He is always portrayed laughing, with a big belly and his finger pointing to the moon. A keen seeker once asked him:

'I have studied the Abhidhamma Pitaka Buddhist scriptures for years yet there are still areas that I do not quite understand. Please could you enlighten me?'

Hotei replied, 'I am illiterate. But if you read it to me I will help uncover their meaning.'

The seeker said, 'But if you can't read them, how can you possibly understand their meaning!'

Hotei pointed to the moon. 'Truth is the moon. Words are the finger. The finger can point to the moon, but the finger is not the moon. To see the moon you have to look beyond the finger.'

In the aftermath of Tim's death there were no fingers pointing anywhere. And even if there were, I would not have been able to see them. I was groping blindly in a dark night with no moon and not even starlight.

For a year I did little other than gaze into the darkness of death and listen to the sounds of silence. I opened my mind beyond my intellect to the possibility of realities in other dimensions. I began to hear and see things beyond the frontiers of my mind, on the edge of my consciousness. Sometimes I thought my grief was driving me insane, other times that I was finding Tim again. Gradually I began to see the invisible moon, the half that never faces Earth and stares into the blackness of deep space, the dark side of the moon.

The second day of Tim's death I sit in bed and drink my tea. I have woken to a world with no sun. My son is dead.

Suddenly Tim is on the end of the bed. I see him clearly. How can this be?

His hand reaches out to hold mine.

'I am so sorry, Mum, I didn't know what I was doing.'

I hear the words. I also hear the depth of sorrow in them. I place my other hand over his.

'I know, Tim, you didn't know what you were doing.'

In the silence, a lifetime falls in on itself. His tiny fingers feeling the air after his birth, his baby arms reaching out for me, his first steps, his falls, his childhood pains, his achievements, our laughter and fun, our struggles and reconciliations, our entanglement and our love, all come down into this moment. Our memories collapse into an intensity so profound it could crack open mountains. We both know this is the last time we will sit together like this.

'I am so, so sorry, Mum.'

'I know, Tim. I know.'

I am saying that I love and understood him so completely there is nothing to say. We have anyway, long before, said what needed to be said between us. The accumulated hostilities and struggles between a son and his mother have been gone through and are long gone. In the stillness of that moment is nothing but love.

Tim is saying sorry for the pain he knows I will go through in his death. He is also telling me of his sorrow at leaving life. He has lost everything. This is his goodbye to it all. Just as it is my goodbye to my precious son. He knows how much I love him, and I know how much he loves me. This knowledge is our last gift to each other.

It is time for Tim to leave. There are more goodbyes to be said on his long farewell to life. I stroke his hand. 'Goodbye, Tim. I love you.' And he is gone.

I sit alone in the early morning silence. A robin sings. Cows graze on the far hill. Two small spiders climb outside the window towards the same web. White clouds drift by.

There is also in these last words a completion of another kind; it is a reflection of the many conversations we'd had in which we talked about his childhood, about the times I had put my search for truth, freedom, God, enlightenment, whatever name I gave what I was seeking, before him. I had said time and time again, 'I am so sorry, Tim, I didn't know what I was doing.' And he had replied just as I had, 'I know, Mum. You didn't know what you were doing.'

When we know a person we love is dying, we say goodbye with love before they die, but Tim and I did not have time before his death to sit together, perhaps wordlessly holding hands, perhaps expressing the hope that we would one day meet again in some other form, perhaps going over his life and honouring the legacy he would leave behind. Tim died suddenly and we did not have the chance. Yet we went through a similar process even though one of us was still in the body and the other had left it. Death is not a single event, it is a process; and heartfelt goodbyes between people who love each other seem to be an intrinsic part of this. Tim said goodbye to many people that day and they said their goodbye to him.

Jo felt Tim come behind her, enfold her in his arms and pour his love into her. John, his father, was driving, and suddenly there was Tim in the car seat next to him. Many of his friends had similar experiences where Tim was suddenly with them, leaning back on the sofa, walking with them down the street, peering over their shoulder at the computer screen. And they felt their love.

When the long goodbye was over, Tim was truly dead.

A National Opinion Poll of 1,467 randomly chosen Americans found that 27% said they had been in direct contact with someone who had died. A scientific survey of over 1,000 people in Iceland found a third claimed to have had contact with the dead. In the UK, Dewi Rees found nearly half of the widows and widowers he interviewed had had experiences of contact with their dead partner. The most common phenomenon was to experience their presence; less common was to see, hear and be touched, though still widespread. He published his results in the *British Medical Journal*, a paper entitled 'The Hallucinations of Widowhood'. But whether we call such experiences hallucinations, comforting fantasies, communications with the dead, the continuation of our relationship in spirit or just wishful thinking, such experiences are accepted without question in many cultures and widespread even in our modern more materialist culture.

Peter and Elizabeth Fenwick report that their research found such experiences were commonly reported not only by spouses, but also by people who had other close relationships, parents and children, grandparents and grandchildren particularly. They write: 'Hallucinations of the bereaved map on to a whole new area of human anecdote and legend – of ghosts, of mediumship – which is way beyond the scope of this book (*The Art of Dying*) to either explore or explain. This is tiger country for scientists, but intriguing nonetheless.'

When your only child dies, it is more than intriguing.

Zeus' sister, Demeter, presided over the sacred law, the cycles of life and death and the fertility of the Earth. A very significant goddess, who, with her daughter Persephone, was a central figure in the Eleusinian Mysteries. If Demeter were not kept happy and continually appeased, the Earth would become a wasteland and the people would starve. Hades, the god of death and the underworld, fell in love with Persephone, seized her and took her into his underworld kingdom. Utterly distraught, Demeter searched for her daughter. All considerations fell away in her grief and so the crops failed and she caused a terrible drought. The people starved. Zeus, with the enlightened self-interest befitting the King of the gods, saw that if this continued, it would deprive the gods of the sacrifice and worship that was their due; he therefore allowed Persephone to return to her mother, but only for part of the year. Winter is when Persephone has to return to the underworld, and once again Demeter's grief renders the Earth infertile and nothing grows.

The landscape of myth is a map of humanity. When Tim died, I too was distraught, searching in my grief everywhere for my lost child. I left my daily life behind, I stopped my work, my social life, my habitual routines, and for a year had few conversations about anything other than death. I abandoned my old life, and set off on a pilgrimage into death, into the underworld, wherever it was my son had gone. I was not going to let death separate me from Tim. I was going to find him even if this meant I would have to die too; my old life was gone anyway. And like Demeter I would not stop my search until I found my son again.

I would spare myself nothing on this quest. I was willing to suffer whatever was the truth. And if this meant first I had to know the absolute and utter finality of death, then I would face up to that. Especially as that was my experience – in all directions, my beloved Tim was completely gone. And nothing and no one could ease that terrible loss. This was my induction into the dreadful knowledge that death is the end of the world, the end of this person, this human being, this animal body that once moved and breathed, the end of all that exists in the dimensions of space and time – literally every thing.

Temporary literally means 'of time'; death is the end of all that exists in time. Death is our time in the chrysalis, the dark night of the soul that burns away what was temporary, destroying the body that lived in time. Fear dies, the fight for survival dies, our defences die, our ego dies, all that was identified with this body dies.

The caterpillar knows only the chrysalis, which is why death is such an utter finality, the complete ending of our life. Certainly for the caterpillar it is the end. And some may never emerge from the chrysalis. Some may be suspended in the darkness for aeons. Others may slip through to the far side of death more quickly. Death is the days of darkness in the tomb before we rise again. Death is when we have lost all sight and cannot yet 'see' in a new way. Death is the loss of our humanity before we become whatever is our next destiny. In one of D H Lawrence's last poems before he died, *The Ship of Death*, he describes death as 'the longest journey' where 'there is nowhere to go, only the deepening blackness darkening still blacker upon the soundless, ungurgling flood, darkness at one with darkness.'

However conscious, enlightened or unafraid one might be, no one escapes his or her encounter with the dark and absolute totality that is death. Yet darkness has its own secrets. Darkness is not only annihilation. Darkness holds a sensitivity, a timelessness, a velvet touch of something other. And like the Hubble telescope, if we wait long enough, we begin to see in that darkness something happens when we die that is not only a fall into the eternal night of oblivion.

A Zen Buddhist meditation, Zazen, involves looking at a blank wall without moving for weeks at a time. Some monks do this for years with only short breaks for eating, sleeping, washing, exercise etc. First they see nothing, just the blank wall. Then they begin to see amazing colours, spirits and wonderful visions. As the meditation deepens, they return to seeing the blank wall. But this time they are seeing the emptiness within which it all happens. Walls and visions, transcendence and ego, struggle and surrender, all happen within one's own awareness. Even death takes place within the context of one's awareness. And it is the very looking that creates this awareness.

When we look into the dark emptiness of death, like the Hubble telescope and monks doing Zazen, gradually our sight adjusts and we begin to see into that darkness. Eventually we begin to see the emptiness of pure awareness itself, the consciousness within which everything happens, including death. This is one way to see into the dark night of death, to make friends with emptiness through meditation. But it is not the only way.

Meditations such as Zazen help prepare us for death by connecting us with pure consciousness, which is very different from the rest of our lives where we are seeking not an empty life but one full of good things, family, friends, activities, achievements, fun, holidays, whatever is our version of happiness. Though if we do not fancy doing time as a Zen monk there's nothing to worry about – we can party, have fun, fall in love, fall out of love, succeed, fail, whatever, because we will encounter loss and emptiness anyway. One thing in life is certain – death.

Ikkyu, the Zen master, was very clever even as a boy. His teacher had a precious teacup, a rare antique. Ikkyu happened to break this cup and was very worried about what he had done. Hearing the footsteps of his teacher, he held the pieces of the cup behind him. The master appeared.

'Why do people have to die?' asked Ikkyu.

'Death is natural,' explained the older man. 'Everything has to die.'

Ikkyu produced the shattered cup.

'Master, it was time for your cup to die.'

There is no way to avoid the emptiness of loss. It will always find us in the end, often on the road we took to avoid it. One day we will no longer be able to turn away and fill it. Even if we delay our encounter to the very end, there is no escape. We can turn away from life, love, freedom, truth, so many things, but we cannot turn away from death. Perhaps, as with all our fears, when we finally turn round and face what we have been running from, we will find there was never anything to fear in the first place – except our fear. Like life, like every moment, like every step we take, death is a journey into the unknown. And it may not be what we fear – just as it may not be what we hope.

Historians well know, the meaning of an event never has an end; it resonates through history. A person is also an event, an event spread out over a lifetime. This event also never has an end. It affects other events that then affect other events and so on ad infinitum. As Lawrence wrote later in the same poem, 'Death is the end... And yet out of eternity a thread separates itself on the blackness, a horizontal thread that fumes a little with pallor upon the dark.' Or as Shunryu Suzuki said more succinctly, which as a Zen Master he would: 'We die; and we do not die.'

2

Manoeuvres in the Dark

A man can die but once; we owe God a death.
Shakespeare, *Henry IV Part II*

Stars were once points of light, pinpricks in a vast darkness. Then we built telescopes and those pinpricks became swirling galaxies, supernova, starfields and giant molecular clouds. Meanwhile, at the other end of existence, atoms were once the smallest indivisible units of matter, until we discovered each atom is a complexity of quarks, leptons and bosons, subatomic particles that may not even be particles at all, but charges of energy or vibrations flashing in and out of existence continually. Both the vast and the infinitesimal have been revealed as more complex than we ever imagined. Material reality is no longer the solid and dependable 'rock' it used to be; it is now uncertain, complex and mysterious. The more we look into death, the more it too becomes complex and mysterious.

No singular belief or idea can encompass the many faces of either life or death. If light can behave as either a wave or a particle, Schrödinger's cat can be both alive and dead until we open the box, and our observations can create the very quantum events we observe, then contradictory experiences and beliefs of death may each hold an aspect of the complexity that is death.

Two Taoists were walking through a field.
  'Death is a gateway to another realm,' said one.
  'You are not dead,' said the other, 'so you do not know if death is a gateway or not.'
  'You are not me,' replied the first, 'so how do you know that I do not know that death is a gateway to another realm.'

'But how do you know I am not you?' asked the other.
'The same way I know death is a gateway to another realm,'
replied the first.

Nietzsche wrote: 'Convictions are more dangerous enemies of truth than lies.' Perhaps especially when exploring the unknowns of death and dying, our beliefs prevent us appreciating the complexity of death. Certainly we are limited when we listen only to what someone else has told us rather than our own experience. To comprehend even a fraction of the complexities of death we need to let death speak to us directly. And death does not speak in comfortable certainties, it is speaks to us only in the vulnerability of experience and in the 'cloud of unknowing'. And when someone we love dies, we learn different things about death than when we just read and think about it.

We begin to see what lies beyond the intellectual mind, where, as the Surangama Sutra tells us, 'things are not what they seem, but neither are they otherwise'. And this kind of experiential exploration reveals the explorer as well as the explored. When we gaze deeply into anything, not only atoms and stars, the one looking is also revealed as more mysterious and complex than we imagined. We begin to realise that what we thought was a singular 'me' is really a 'we'. Walt Whitman wrote, 'Do I contradict myself? Very well, then I contradict myself. I am large, I contain multitudes.' Not only Whitman, each of us contains a multitude.

Along with atoms and stars, each of us is not a single indivisible unit but a complexity composed of many parts. Within us lie communities of selves, sub-personalities, inner beings, archetypes, energies, contradictory and opposing impulses and drives. In each of us lives a child, a parent, a controller, a risk taker, one who fears freedom, one who is not afraid, a ruthless survivor, a generosity that does not think of itself, a wise person, a shadowy trickster, a silent witness, a warrior, an infinity of possibilities. Though just as certain plants grow only in a particular climate, each one of us can embody only aspects of the infinite in a single life – in that is our uniqueness.

We are unique and complex creatures and this is reflected in the uniqueness and complexity of our deaths. When we die, every part of us goes on that great journey, and each aspect that came to life within us also dies, undergoing its own journey into the mystery that is death.

A complex life involves a complex death; a simple life involves a simple death. Though what may appear as a simple life can have hidden complexities within the person, just as what may appear to be a complex life can have an inner simplicity, and it is the inner reality that determines the nature of one's death. As Ralph Waldo Emerson wrote: 'What is inside us and hidden while we are alive becomes apparent and all of reality when we are dead.'

There are many stories of how Masters from Hindu, Tibetan and Buddhist traditions died gracefully. The Zen Master Goei burned incense, sat in meditation posture and told his disciples, 'I am going.' A monk asked him, 'Where are you going?' Goei replied, 'No place.' The monk asked, 'Will I be able to see you?' Goei said, 'Where I am going cannot be seen by human eyes.' Then he closed his eyes and peacefully passed away. Telanga Swami was a Hindu Swami who, to the continual consternation of the Varanasi police, was always naked. A month before he died he announced his work was finished and told his disciples the date he would be leaving this life. He ordered a coffin to be made and on the appointed day blessed his disciples and admirers, climbed into the coffin and sat in full lotus position for meditation. It was some time before anyone realised he was not in the still silence of meditation but had died. Neem Karoli Baba called his disciples together one day and told them, 'Today, I am released from Central Jail forever.' Later that day he was rushed into hospital with what was diagnosed as a diabetic coma. He woke up in the emergency room and said, 'Hail to the Master of the Universe,' several times, and peacefully died.

A simple death is seen in the East as a manifestation of enlightenment and we might imagine that this is the kind of death we should be aiming for. But Eastern gurus and Masters are part of less individualised traditions; they hold the enlightenment for the rest of the community while it engages with the struggle for survival and the business of the world. Our modern psyches are more complex. In our world, we have great individual freedom, and this means most of us have to engage the worldly *and* the spiritual, the fight with death *and* the surrender. And so for us, death is not a singular event, serenely entered into in full lotus; it is a journey into the unknown in which different parts of us experience that journey differently – some aspects might serenely die peacefully, others might refuse to go so gently into that night and will 'rage against the dying of the light'. So for us, unlike the Masters of the East, our death is likely to involve a variety of experiences in which different parts of us die differently. Certainly in my experience with Tim there were many different journeys to be made before he finally dissolved into the cosmos forever. And some were not anything like I had expected.

The day after Tim died, Martin and I drive to London. I see people walking around, laughing, gossiping, shopping, calling out to their children, joking with friends. I no longer belong in this world. I am in an invisible purdah with a veil between me and everything. My son is dead. I no longer belong anywhere. Except to death. I belong to death.

I am determined to see Tim's body as soon as I can. I would have gone straight to the morgue if I could, but it is not open until 9 am the next day. The coroner has told everyone that we must wait to see the body in the funeral parlour. Apparently the morgue is not the right setting to see his body before he has been made to look 'respectable'. I don't care what the setting is. Or what Tim's body looks like. Besides Tim was not respectable. Yet Tim's body has become property of the state and the coroner has the right to refuse to let me see it. But I will see my son. I will walk past armed guards with machine guns and they can shoot me down – I am going to my son's body.

Monday morning at 9 am exactly, I call the coroner. Perhaps he hears something in my voice because he says, 'Of course. Come at 11 am and we will have the body ready for you to view.'

Martin and I arrive early. I pace around a small park nearby, consumed by an overwhelming sense of urgency. At 10.55 am, Martin and I walk into the morgue. I am not met by the pull-out drawer I am expecting, they have put the body in a private room and leave us alone. Tim lies in a body bag unzipped to his waist, his hands and arms outside it. He looks asleep. For a wild moment I expected him to wake up and laugh, saying – tricked you! But I touch his cheek and it is cold. Colder than the frozen wastes of the Arctic. Colder than the endless night of deep space. As cold as death.

'Oh Tim! Oh Tim!' I lean over and kiss his forehead. I stroke his head. My tears fall on to his face and roll down his cheek on to his neck. I bend over and weep the inconsolable tears of a mother over her dead son. I abandon myself to this grief.

Suddenly I sense Tim in the room. I feel his essence, his spirit, his presence, his energy, but whatever I call this Tim, it is not his body. That is lying cold on the table.

'Tim is here,' I said to Martin.

'Yes, I feel him too.'

I can sense that Tim now knows he was dead, but is uncertain – if this body is not him, then who or what is he? Despite not having the slightest idea what is going on, I know exactly what to say. 'This body was once you,' I say aloud, 'but it is no longer you. You are now a spirit. We who love you, we are now your body in the world.'

I sense Tim listening and continue. 'Your body can rest now. It no longer has to suffer anguish or pain ever again. You are now a spirit, free to be the brilliant, funny, unique spirit you have always been, but *without the constraints of a physical body.'*

I feel Tim begin to realise that having no body could be a new adventure. And without the weight of a body to pull him down with gravity, his spirit does not have to hang around the body that was once who he was; he can move, explore and play as the spirit he now is.

I tell him: 'We are your body now. When I am walking in the fells and looking up at the mountains, you will be looking through my eyes. When Jo is swimming, you will be swimming too. When Nabil is making music you will be making music with him. And when Chris is cracking jokes and having fun, you will be laughing too.'

Martin says, 'And when I am struggling with accounts, your spirit can struggle to do accounts with me!'

Suddenly there is an explosive release. A rush of energy like an ecstatic whirlwind fills the room with an overwhelming sense of playful freedom. The unique Tim-ness we know so well begins to laugh with delight and dance around, playing as pure energy. Martin and I stand speechless. We cannot comprehend what is happening. This tim-ness is dancing with joy about the room, with an intensity and power that is inexplicable yet undeniable.

On the third day, Tim has risen from the dead. And I am encountering a mystery beyond my comprehension.

The attendant at the morgue knocks on the door to let us know our half hour is up. He holds the door open for us. 'I am sorry for your loss,' he says. 'Thank you,' I say. I am more than normally grateful, but this is not the time to tell him that even in the depths of my sorrow something glorious has happened – my son has risen from the dead. Instead we bow our heads to the great god of death and Martin and I leave. We go out into the sun. And Tim comes with us.

We walked by the canal along the Lea River valley, two in the body, one in the spirit. We could not hug each other or link arms, but we could sense and feel each other, exactly as if Tim were with us. We watched birds. We listened to the distant roar of London. We laughed together as we had so many times over the years. And we wondered at this unexpected strangeness.

I had thought I also had died. I had imagined I would be under the ground, shrouded in darkness, never to laugh or play again, all life gone from me forever, that this death was the end of not only Tim, but the end of me too. I had believed that when we die, the person dies with the body and we dissolve into the cosmos. Maybe whatever transcendental qualities we have cooked up on Earth, such as love, wisdom, consciousness, beauty or whatever, continue to exist, but impersonally so because the person is no more. Yet even while Tim's body lay cold and dead in the morgue, his unique spirit was alive, dancing about with delight and intimately connected with us.

Is there really a soul, 'a pale ghost', a 'fuming thread' or a dancing laughing energy that survives our death? Or is the idea of a soul merely a projection of our human longing for transcendence, and the true spirit of that person lives on only in the hearts and memories of those still living? Or are descriptions of communication with spirits a form of our continued relationship with them? After all, they may have died but our love for them does not.

I have spoken with many people who are curious, enquiring and open to dialogue in many areas but as soon as we come to death, they become dogmatic. 'You go to the light.' 'You have a life review and see your mistakes.' 'You choose another reincarnation.' 'You become a spirit.' 'All spirits are essentially seeking truth.' And so on. When I ask what makes them think like this, they explain that this is what they believe is true. But as Friedrich Nietzsche pointed out: 'Belief means not wanting to know what is true.' And when it comes to understanding death we have to be willing to question our beliefs.

Yet it is very difficult to challenge our own beliefs.

It seems to be our human nature to tell ourselves stories and then believe it is reality. We could say the whole of human culture is a story we have collectively agreed to tell ourselves. Yet the only reality we can assert with any authority has its roots in our direct experience, all else is a repeated story from someone else's direct experience. So when we believe something, we do not truly know, we just *think* we know. This is especially tricky when we explore death because beliefs abound about what happens when we die – even though those beliefs, however dogmatic, tend to be very different.

It helps to understand that spiritual, humanistic and psychological explanations appear to be describing incompatible realities when really they are speaking of the same phenomena in different languages. One difficulty is the difference between the languages of mythology and the languages of *Logos*.

Logos is the logical, pragmatic, scientific kind of thinking needed to organise society and develop technologies in the material world. The *Logos* of science, which is the dominant explanatory paradigm of our modern culture, might dismiss myths as fantasies, but this is a misunderstanding. A myth is not a story; it imparts a different kind of knowledge. Mythological thinking deals with the sacred archetypes of society and the meaning of humanity's role in the cosmos. Myth and *Logos*, therefore, have separate and complementary jobs to do. We need both.

The forces of nature that keep our species alive, our instincts, are in opposition to the forces of society that make us human, our conditionings. This conflict comes into sharp focus when we look at death. Our instincts will kill in an instant to survive; our humanity will try to maintain life at all costs. This conflict is deep within our human psyche, and we need help to live with these contradictory impulses at war within us. One of the primary functions of Myth is to help us live with the existential predicament that to become human is to enter into a war with oneself.

Logos enables us to protect and defend ourselves from death, to survive, to create comfortable lives with a degree of security and safety. Myths help us deal with the existential suffering that we live on an Earth where the Law of the Jungle is 'eat or be eaten', the terrible underpinning of all life, that for each one of us to live, something else has to die. This conflict is at the heart of all ritual. Ultimately, death is the only resolution. As Plato wrote, 'Only the dead have seen the end of war.' Which is why death is at the heart of all mythology.

Myth and death are intimately interconnected in all cultures. To access the sacred knowledge contained within a myth the initiate has to symbolically die. Shamans all over the world enter altered states of consciousness to access the Spirit World in order to harness the healing powers and knowledge of that realm. But to enter the spirit realm you have to die. In all traditions, the training to be a shaman involves an experience of death. The secret ceremonies of the Eleusinian Mysteries involved ritually dying in order to go beyond your fear of death and, in doing so, you were liberated from the constraints imposed by society on our instincts. In many societies boys are taken from their mothers to undergo a gruelling ritual initiation into manhood that involves a ritual death. This is because for a boy to become a man he has to become willing to die in order to protect the tribe – and there is no way through our fear of death other than to experience it.

In a sacred ritual we are initiated into the knowledge that there are more important things for a human being than animal survival. Freedom, justice, honour, the spirit of genuine enquiry, the children of a community that contain its future, the creation of beauty, integrity, the balance of nature, love, these all matter more than an individual's survival. When survival comes at the expense of these qualities, we destroy what matters more than any individual life. As Robert Ingersoll expressed it: 'I would rather live and love where death is king than have eternal life where love is not.' And you can only learn this through some kind of experience of death itself. We learn the meaning of life through death.

In an interview with the *Guardian*, Anthony Hopkins described life, 'We're all just a bunch of sinners crashing around in the darkness.' This may be the myth of a Hollywood that creates its own mythology of fame in order to make money but the true myths of a society contain understandings that make life far more than this. Myths hold sacred knowledge. And when a society loses its connection with its myths and the deeper currents within itself, it loses its soul.

We might define the soul as the essential quality of a person or society, its being-ness, its unique meaning; but however we define 'soul', to lose one's soul is a terrible fate. As Plato wrote, 'Death is not the worst that can happen to us.' Myths teach us the sacred knowledge that to lose one's soul is a far worse fate than death. And they do this through symbolic rituals of death.

An instinctive fear of death is natural, it keeps us alive; but the kind of terror that leads us to sacrifice what makes life worth living, in order to have a life that is not therefore worth having, is different. Our own terror can kill our soul in a kind of inner terrorism. Myths, and the rituals that align us to them, take us to the far side of death so that although we still have a natural fear of death, we are no longer terrified of it. We ritually cross the threshold of death in a transition from the mundane to the sacred, and this is the end of our terror of death.

D W Winnicott wrote, 'The death we fear is the death we have already experienced.' He meant that we project on to death all the fears we have not yet resolved within ourselves. Death then becomes the objectification of all that we dread. The actual reality of death is not what we truly fear at all, yet we can only discover this through a conscious death in ritual symbolic form. Then we are no longer afraid of death because we know it.

Once we have known death, we will never again betray the

deeper meaning of life by sacrificing our soul for mere bodily survival. We understand that death is part of life not separate from it. We are initiated into the open secret at the core of all true spirituality – that our lives can be greater than our deaths.

Though it is up to us whether we have the courage to come fully alive and therefore have a meaningful death or turn both into non-events. Bertolt Brecht wrote, 'Do not fear death so much, but rather the inadequate life.' It is, after all, life that teaches us how to die. And we cannot die well when we live in a fear of death. Yet when the fear of death is in us yet we are not in the fear, then as well as the fearful parts of us, there are many other parts that are not afraid to die for what we love. This love is what makes our lives greater than our deaths.

The function of sacred myths is to free us from being imprisoned in a fear of death, in order that we can truly love life. True spirituality is not the empty rituals in churches and temples; it is when we love life enough to become unafraid of death.

In our modern world, an initiation into the sacred tends to come, not through religious ritual or collective initiation, but through a more individual and personal route. For example when someone we love dies, we lose all our money, become chronically ill, our pet dies, we make a dreadful mistake, a friend moves away, each of these events involves a kind of death. Any kind of death, from a loss of one's job to a painful divorce, is an invitation into the sacred, if we so choose. And no one steps into the river of death and emerges unchanged. Death transforms us.

Tim's death was my initiation into new understandings of the sacred because it was a death for me too. Certainly the mother in me died, I have no other children. But not only the mother died, my old life disintegrated. I was forced to encounter new dimensions of myself. I had to re-examine my beliefs and question myself on every level. I had to let the searing experience of my loss teach me that in the end, *how* we die matters more than *that* we die. And I had to learn this through a personal experience of death because the myths and rituals offered to me by religion sounded hollow and empty and did not speak to me.

Organised religions used to be the vessels for the sacred in society but no longer. For a start, they have their teachings embedded in hierarchical cultures very different from the individualistic one we now inhabit. We do not live like a cardinal in the 15th century Vatican or a monk in 12th century Tibet. We need to explore death with our current understandings of human nature and the workings of the universe because then we can find our place in the cosmos and our relationship to life and death, not according to mediaeval maps drawn up long ago, according to how we live now. For example, the ultimate authority to which we are answerable in our modern world is not an external deity; it is our own integrity. 'God is dead,' as Nietzsche told us.

The evolution from an authoritarian religion to a self-determining humanism does not mean our modern life has no sacred river running through. But it does mean the sacred has to be found now by each individual and we must find our own way through the labyrinth. Where once tribal ritual, church dogma or community history gave us the meaning of our lives and deaths, now we have to find this for ourselves. And the myths that speak to us are very different from those that spoke to our ancestors.

A myth of death that we create for ourselves, that gives meaning to life, is not a spiritual belief or religious dogma, it is a living truth that informs and inspires us, that orders our actions, that determines how we relate with each other. The myth we align ourselves behind determines how we live, and therefore how we will die, and this may be very different from our proclaimed religion or belief of God. For example, fundamental Christians who dogmatically demonise others dwell in a far more primitive myth than Christianity. Just as many atheists in a struggle for authenticity and truth may be living with a far more spiritual narrative than they imagine.

Some people might write their myth using the template of a heaven complete with saints and angels. Others might turn to the maps of our human psyche and have the dead live in our hearts and memories. Others might prefer a scientific paradigm and speak of vibrations and energy fields, or might use New Age terminology and speak of the continuous creation of reality through our thoughts. Some might use Eastern ideas of reincarnation and speak of the evolution of individual consciousness through lifetimes; others might speak of the spirit of that person and the ways in which that lives on in life, in the legacy of their work, in memories, in the lasting contributions they made to our lives. And, when someone we love dies, we may find we need more than one template to give meaning to our experiences. We may even need to invent new ones completely.

After WW1 there was a craze for Ouija boards and spiritualism. Millions of people were grieving loved ones but had no body to say goodbye to and ritually bury; they had to find their new relationship with the dead through other means than traditional funerals and mourning. Spiritualism and new descriptions of life after death emerged. In WW2 we witnessed the awful depths of our human capacity for darkness. We saw that hell is not something after death, it is something we create here on Earth. The suffering and losses of 80 million deaths created new understandings and consciousness, and a new humanism emerged, which reclaimed the soul of humanity from religion and placed it in the sphere of our political and personal actions.

In my first vivid dream I encountered my deepest terror, and found death was nothing to fear after all. In another vivid dream I encountered death in a different way.

I am standing in front of an enormous diamond, cut with thousands of facets and as tall as a house. It spins on an ever-rotating axis, continually presenting me with a different face. I am told I am looking at the

35

Vajra Diamond of Truth. I remember that 'vajra' means 'diamond' in Tibetan, and in Buddhism, the vajra truth is the Diamond Truth that cannot be destroyed. Each face of this diamond confronts me with a reality that cannot be destroyed nor argued with, because what faces me, in that moment, is the absolute truth. Then the diamond rotates and presents me with another absolute truth, but which flatly contradicts the truth before.

I stare into the ultimate truth that upon death we return to the source and dissolve into the one-ness. I then stare into another ultimate truth, that after death our unique essence, our being-ness remains in some form or other for eternity. The great diamond spins again. When we die we are gone forever and cease to exist at all. It spins again. When we die we remain alive in spirit for always. Another face shows me the death of someone we love is an absolute and inconsolable loss. Yet another reveals death is a liberation and a release from all suffering. The diamond continues to spin, facet after facet revealing itself. Death finds its meaning in us, in life. Death has a meaning that is a mystery for the living. Death is in life, here and now, every moment. Death does not exist in the moment, only in time. Death is a final and absolute ending. Death is the gateway to eternity. The remorseless diamond spins on. Tim's death is a tragedy. Tim's death has a mysterious meaning. Tim's death is the cause of great suffering. Tim's death is a release from all suffering. The great pitiless Vajra-diamond of truth continues to spin. I am responsible for Tim's death. Our family history is responsible. Tim alone is responsible. No one is responsible, it happened. My responsibility lies in how I live with this. How I live with it is not the point, how I die with it is.

I scrabble to make sense of it all. But the Vajra-diamond doesn't care that such paradoxical opposites are impossible to reconcile. Reality is all of it.

Not only is death a complex process in which different parts of us die differently, a grief too is complex, with many challenges and experiences in which different parts of us grieve differently. My grief was my initiation into the sacred mysteries of death because Tim's death was also my death. The old me died. If you look at your life and all the 'deaths' that you have experienced, you are likely to see how these also initiated you into different understandings and new ways of being. This is because death reaches into parts of us that no success, joy, fulfilment, hope, delight, or any kind of living the dream can.

We might even discover in our encounters with death that, hidden behind what we feared, is what we long for. And when the time comes and we also sail in our ship of death on that last voyage, we may find, in the vastness of that mystery, there was never anything to fear all along.

3

The Question With No Answer

A student went to a Zen Master and asked:
'What happens after death?'
The Master replied: 'I don't know.'
'But you're an enlightened Master!' protested the student.
'Yes, but not a dead one.'

The only certainty in life is death. There may be few correspon-
dences between the lives of a Chinese politician, a native of the
Amazonian jungle, a Wall Street banker and a single mother in a
Manchester housing estate, but they have one thing in common –
whatever our lives, we will all die. Whatever our beliefs about
death, whether we believe death is an oblivion, an awakening, an
ending or a transformation, death itself is a reality we cannot
avoid. And whether we look for the meaning of death in our
earthly existence, in our human realm, or seek meaning in a
transcendental dimension beyond this realm, death renders life
almost unbearably meaningful. Any exploration of life, therefore,
has to include an exploration of death.

Death is intrinsic to life. If we did not die, we would not be
driven to create anything and freedom would become worthless.
Death ensures that each moment matters. We might think we
want to live forever but what would happen when we had done
it all, lived it all, experienced it all, and yet continued to live here
on Earth? There would be no surprises, no creativity nor
challenge of any kind and we would be locked into a hell of
banality, boredom and meaninglessness. We would soon long for
the release of death. As Socrates wrote: 'Death may be the
greatest of all human blessings.' We tend to think that life is
wonderful and death terrible, but death shows us that life is

wonderful, yes, but also terrible, just as death is terrible, yes, but also wonderful. Quite simply life would have no meaning without death.

Though how do we explore death when we are not yet dead?

But death is all around us. The First Law of the Jungle is 'eat or be eaten'. The birth of one thing inevitably involves the death of something else. When someone we love dies, a part of us dies too. Any major change in our lives such as an accident, a chronic illness, an animal we love dying, winning the lottery, the birth of a child, each involves a death to aspects of who we were before. We can explore death and our hopes and fears of dying while alive, if for no other reason than learning about death teaches us about life. As Epicurus wrote, 'The art of living well and the art of dying well are one.'

Many traditions and cultures throughout history have understood that life and death are not antagonistic opposites but interdependent realities in which each takes its significance from the other. The Sufi secret for wisdom was to know that 'this too will pass.' The Zen teaching said to guarantee enlightenment in one lifetime was to live as if death would arrive the next moment. Jack Kerouac's advice on how to be truly creative was: 'accept loss forever.' These perspectives recognise that our place in the cosmos, the evolution of our consciousness and our psycho-spiritual destinies are to be found in death as much as in life. As Friedrich Nietzsche wrote: 'Let us beware of saying that death is the opposite of life. The living being is only a species of the dead, and a very rare species.' But despite that death is in the heart of our lives, we rarely think or talk about death.

Perhaps this is natural. Apart from the fact that we cannot know what happens when we die because we are not dead, the last thing we want to think about while struggling to make a good life for ourselves is that, one day, all this will end. It is a paradox: while we now have access to more information about life than previous generations, literally in the palm of our hands on our smart phones and tablets, at the same time we have less understanding of death. Death in our modern world happens in hospitals and hospices not in our homes. Our medical technologies mean we expect to survive the diseases and accidents that killed most of our ancestors. We buy our food in shops, we do not hunt and kill it. Many of us have never even seen a dead body. We are protected from the harsh realities of death and imagine we will die in some far away future when we are very old and probably won't mind 'shuffling off the mortal coil.' As Andrew Rooney said, 'Death is a distant rumour to the young.'

As a consequence, when most of us think of death, we tend to make assumptions about what happens based on mediaeval Christian myths or descriptions of death from very different societies such as ancient Tibet, rural India or diverse aboriginal cultures. We may populate our version of an afterlife with ancestors and angels. We may conjure up scenes of travelling through the bardos as described in Tibetan Buddhism. We may conceive that we are reborn as a fish or a king depending on our karma, float on clouds playing harps, be entertained by thousands of virgins, or dissolve into the light 'of a thousand suns.' Yet whatever the spiritual language we use to describe death, it will have had its roots in the culture that gave rise to it. We live in very different times. Our experiences of death and dying will not be the same as those of a Chinese Empress, a feudal peasant, a mediaeval Cardinal or a 12th century Tibetan Lama, simply because our experience of being alive is different.

To understand death in our modern age, therefore, we cannot rely on old myths; we need to draw new spiritual maps of our place in the cosmos and the meaning of our humanity, ones relevant to who we have become in modern times. We are all human but our experience of that humanity is dependent upon many variables.

Shin Dong-hyuk was born in one of the political concentration camps of North Korea where he lived with unimaginable torture and abuse. He is the only prisoner ever to have escaped the most repressive 'total control zone' camp. In an interview he was asked if he was happy to be free. He looked blank and then explained that growing up with torture and abuse on a daily basis had made it impossible for him ever to be happy, that is not what his life was about. His life, he said, was not about himself at all, it was about letting the world know what was going on inside these terrible places. It was the interviewer's turn to look blank. She could not imagine a life in which seeking personal happiness was irrelevant.

We tend to assume that our modern experience of identity, which is primarily linked to being a particular individual, is a universal experience, yet really it is a phenomenon with psychological and cultural dimensions that have evolved over time. Being human is a cultural event not only a biological one. A North Korean farmer, a Masai warrior and an insurance salesman from Leeds not only lead very different lives externally, their experience of being a person and alive is also different. Death therefore has cultural and psychological dimensions as well as physical and spiritual ones. An exploration of death will have to involve, therefore, an exploration of how our sense of self has developed both historically and ontologically. Especially as, after all, it is the individual who dies, not the society, family or community he or she belonged to.

In our modern world we take it for granted that each individual has an intrinsic worth, yet for most of human history what mattered far more was a person's place and status within the community, their caste or class, their family and tribe. A person's identity was connected with the tribe and nation they belonged to rather than their unique individuality. This affected their experiences of death because when the individual died, the greater collective he or she identified with did not. Our modern identity, on the other hand, is linked more to our unique separate individuality than it is to the class, nation or the family that we belong to. Here is another reason why we find it hard to think about death in modern culture: death is more frightening for us because it holds a more potent finality.

There is a story told by the Zen Master D T Suzuki: One day while out walking a man stumbled upon a vicious tiger. He ran away but soon came to the edge of a high cliff. He turned around and saw the great jaws of the tiger and climbed down a vine that dangled over the precipice. As he swayed over the chasm below clinging desperately to the vine, two mice appeared and began to gnaw through the vine. He looked down into the abyss, and suddenly noticed a wild strawberry growing out of the cliff face. He reached out, picked it and popped it in his mouth. It was absolutely the most delicious strawberry he had ever tasted!

Suzuki said the original ending to this story, however, was quite different. He changed it because he said Westerners would not be able to stomach the original version. In this the strawberry turns out to be deadly poisonous.

It is another paradox: in our culture we have less experience of death than previous generations yet death is far more significant and frightening for us than ever before.

There are other difficulties when we try to explore death. Death has dimensions beyond our human intellect yet when we think and talk about death we cannot help but use intellectual ideas and concepts that have evolved to work within the material dimension of objects separated in space and time, even when we know that aspects of what happens on death are outside this. For example, the very questions we ask when exploring death are tricky. What is death? What happens when we die? Who dies? These are questions using a language that has evolved to deal with a material world consisting of individual objects with their separate existences that interact in some kind of cause and effect matrix. But as Wittgenstein wrote: 'the cause-effect nexus is not really a nexus at all.'

The universe, life and each one of us are events as much as 'things'. Each of us is a happening as much as an individual object. We exist as interconnected relationships as much as independent entities. Certain types of questions, therefore, may look as if they have meaning but really they are distractions and can confuse us when we are exploring events such as consciousness.

Yet we cannot explore death without using our consciousness to explore consciousness itself. Language is therefore necessary. It is further complicated because the very language we use plays a part in actually determining the nature of our experience – as Marshall McLuhan pointed out, 'the medium is the message.' And when we explore consciousness, the nature of experience, self-awareness and other experiential phenomena, we have to use a language that gives the illusion we are describing a particular reality when really we are speaking of our experience. Nowhere is this more apparent than when we explore death.

Death takes us into many apparently contradictory realities because it takes us out of the intellectual mind that creates order and demands facts. This capacity has evolved as a tool for survival but death is a phenomenological event of energy and consciousness, nothing whatsoever to do with our survival. Yet when we speak about the events of death, the language we are forced to use can delude us into thinking we refer to dimensions of reality in the same way we can describe our material world of space and time. Yet we are talking about energy not things, happenings not objects, the formless not form.

For example, we might describe death as a journey into a bright light or a heaven with angels, or as a time of reflection before our next reincarnation, or as a dissolution into the void, and we can forget that we are talking of an experience not an actual reality. We can then easily imagine that angels, gods, white lights and so on are entities that exist as we do. It is like when we dream. We do not actually visit the scenes we see. The descriptions of green fields, city streets or a paradise island that we describe when telling a dream are the linguistic patterns we place on to our experience. Those images are not actual realities with shape and substance but more templates to enable us to understand and communicate our experience.

The terms 'angel', 'light beings', 'God', 'demon' and so on are linguistic tools, metaphors, to communicate our experience; they are personifications of that experience rather than actual realities in shape and form. Angels do not exist as we paint them, think of them and imagine them, yet people who use the word 'angel' can only describe their experience though personifying certain aspects of their experience and speaking as if angels exist. 'Angels' are energies not objects, experiences not actualities, but this does not mean that what we are trying to communicate is less real, or even that angels are not real. It is just as meaningful to argue that angels are as real as atoms, galaxies and any other concept or perceptual construct we have created to articulate our experience.

About six months after Tim had died, my vivid dreams stopped. I missed them. Though of course it was not really the dreams I was missing – it was Tim himself.

I took to reading spiritual books before I went to sleep, hoping their wisdom would seep into my unconscious during the night. Tibetan Rinpoches, Osho, Barry Long, Wittgenstein, Irvin Yalom, Deepak Chopra, Teilhard de Chardin... The pile of books by my bed grew, though not my understanding of death. One night I dipped into Rudolph Steiner and read that we can remain in contact with the dead if, last thing before we sleep, we ask them a question. Our first thought on waking will be their answer. Just before I drifted off, I asked Tim: 'Why do I feel so painfully responsible for your death? And why, given so many wise people say death is a liberation, am I so devastated with grief?'

That night I had another of the vivid dreams.

I am in my bedroom and have dropped my mobile phone. It is broken. Tim is there. I remember how he used to mend things like that for me. 'Give it to me, Mum. I'll fix it.' And he would have done. Or got me a new one if it couldn't be fixed. But now I have to fix it; he is a disembodied tim-ness and cannot deal with the material world of technology and phones. Even in the dream I wonder if this is a sign that I need to mend something in our communication. Tim cannot do it, I have to. I dropped the phone not him.

I stare at my broken phone and realise that recently I have been telling myself that my dreams and imagined conversations with Tim have no reality; they are all in my own mind, fantasies to protect me from the awful totality of his death. I look up at the Tim before me.

'I dropped the phone didn't I?' I say.

'Yes. You did.' He sits on the edge of the bed and lights up a cigarette.

'Hey, what's this? You're a spirit, what are you doing smoking!'

He takes a drag and grins. 'But, Mum, I am free to be anything I wish, a smoker, a joker, a midnight toker. Anything. Just as you are free to see me howsoever you wish.'

'But is this you? Or just random neurones firing in my brain during REM sleep?'

'Well, Mum, think about it, even what we call reality is a creative interpretation of energies.' He takes another drag of his spiritual fag. 'After all, when the energies of different wavelengths of light fall on your eyes and you interpret what you see as a table, a tree or a full moon, that is a human interpretation you've learned. A wolf might see a threat, a den or a sharper shadow in which a goat can hide. Who knows what a fly might see.' He leans back and blows smoke rings. 'Humans create the world one way, wolves another, flies another. And when it comes to interpreting the energies of the dead, well, each one of

us sees into the matrix differently.'

He pushes back his cap, scratches his head. What kind of spirit wears a cap and smokes? I haven't spoken but he says, 'This one,' and stubs out his cigarette on an ashtray that has suddenly appeared. 'Now let's get down to business.' He is suddenly serious. 'Your first question. I can tell you time and time again that there is no trouble between us. We love each other; we both know that. I am dealing with things yes, but not about you. We did all we had to do together. In fact yours and my connection is my major support during this process. But only you can truly take on board that you are OK and that there is nothing but love between us now.' He grins. 'Though it's up to you, Mum. You can interpret this dream how you like.'

'But why be so grief struck when someone dies if death is a liberation not a loss?'

'That's a good question. I wonder what your answer will be.' He puts his arm round my shoulder and hugs me. 'You and I, Mum, we've always done it differently, and here we are still going our own sweet way and getting the dead to channel the living rather than the other way round. I like it!' He grins. 'Let me tune in.'

He sits crossed-legged on the bed and wobbles about pretending to be tuning in on some esoteric broadband and winks at me.

'Here you come... The art of living and dying is to be totally engaged and committed to life while alive and to let it all go in an instant when you die. Some are better at the engagement, others at the letting go. But this means that some parts of you let go easily and can be with me in death, no problem, while other parts, more engaged and committed to life, cannot help but have pain at my death.'

He uncrosses his legs. 'Being dead, of course, I don't have that problem.' He reaches for his cigarettes again. 'I let go into death very quickly, most find they take a while longer to let go of life. That was partly because you helped me.' He grins and takes a toke on what has suddenly become a spliff. 'And partly because I had a lot of practice. Partying hard is a crash course in the art of letting-go!'

He stands up and, as he has ended thousands of our phone conver-

sations before, tells me:

'Got to go, Mum, lots of love.'

I woke up thinking the phone has been mended after all. My doubts had broken the connection and here it was back again. Though whether the connection was with a dead Tim in spirit, a dialogue with the Tim who lives in my heart, a manifestation in dream form of our love, an experience of quantum entanglement, the workings of a transcendentally interconnected energy field, or even random firings of neurones in REM sleep, I couldn't say. Those were all different languages describing the same phenomenon anyway, and I was more interested in the phenomenon itself.

Whatever was happening between and beyond Tim and me, or tim-ness and me, or the unfolding of tim-anne-ness, however it was described, what really mattered to me was that the phone had been mended and the dreams began again. Tim and I loved each other and there was a meeting in these dreams whether imagined or real. As John Keats wrote, 'I am certain of nothing but the holiness of the heart's affections and the truth of imagination.'

But I still wanted to *know* what was happening for Tim, have some kind of proof, something solid to hold on to – even while another part of me recognised this was impossible and really I just wanted him back.

One school of thought suggests that when we die, what happens is up to us, we create our own experience. If we expect to see a bright light we do. If we expect to be judged by God, we are. In a kind of self-fulfilling prophecy, if we expect purgatory, re-incarnation or oblivion then, respectively, that is what we experience. There may be some truth to this; like in life, if we expect something to hurt, we tense ourselves against it and that tension can itself be painful. If we expect people to be friendly, we relax which means people tend to relax and be friendly with us. But this cannot be the whole truth. The cosmos is far greater and more mysterious than whatever I might believe it is – thank goodness. If the human mind can contain reality then all mystery and transcendence is gone. Not knowing leads to a more intimate engagement with reality than knowing.

Not knowing is crucial in an exploration of death, because here we truly do not know what happens when we die – not with our intellectual minds anyway. We literally have no idea. Yet many of the religions of the world describe the events on death as dogma. But dogmatic assertions about what is death stifle genuine dialogue and, like mediaeval arguments about how many angels can fit on to the head of a pin, we can end up inanely arguing about whose version of the afterlife is the right one.

There are no objective answers to questions such as 'what is death?' It is like asking, what is the meaning of life? There can be none because what is being addressed by such questions is a person not an event. There are therefore only the answers each of us chooses to give. If I ask you what is the meaning of life you cannot tell me, but you will be able to say what it is for you, and I will be able to say what it is for me. As well, those answers will be continually changing as we change.

The meaning is not in life and death per se, it is us who give meaning to them. We can use the experience and ideas of others, we can engage in a dialogue with the spiritual languages of other cultures, we can read books and listen to teachers, but in the end it is up to each one of us to create our own understanding of what it means to live and die. And that will be, for each of us, whatever we decide that is. We can even give away our own authority and believe what we are told if we so choose. But there are dangers in this that might not be apparent initially, because when we die, we die alone.

No one dies our death with us. No one can therefore tell us how to die. My death will not be like your death, which will not be like anyone else's death. Our death is our own.

A renowned Zen master said that his greatest teaching was: 'Death is the end of the unique self.'

Profoundly impressed by the profundity of this, one monk decided to leave the monastery and retreat to meditate solely on this insight. For the next twenty years he lived alone in a cave and meditated on this great teaching. One day he met another monk who was traveling through the forest. Quickly the hermit monk learned that the traveller also had studied under the same Zen master. Eagerly he asked: 'Please, tell me what you know of the master's greatest teaching.' The traveller's eyes lit up. 'Ah, the master has been very clear about this. He says that his greatest teaching is this: Death is not the end of the unique self.'

It is up to us to create the meaning of our own death. Liberation is not a serenity beyond duality and anguish, it is far greater than that. It is the freedom to live your own life and die your own death in your own unique way. In the words of Albert Camus, 'There is but one freedom, to put oneself right with death. After that everything is possible.'

4

Soul Music

There's a star-man waiting in the sky,
He'd like to come and meet us,
But he thinks he'll blow our minds.
David Bowie

Historically, both individually and collectively, we have created our gods in our own image. A society inevitably creates its gods, and its demons, in accordance with its own mores and morals. Hunter-gathering societies ate and enjoyed what the earth produced and prayed to mother goddesses to provide for them. The first farmers were more dependent on the weather for their crops than the nomadic tribes, who moved with the warmth rather than creating it, and so agrarian societies worshipped wind, rain and fire gods. In herding societies, such as the Hebrew tribe, you find the one God caring for his flock of chosen souls. The Greek development of democracy and cultural academies in cities was reflected in the community of deities on Mount Olympus. In hierarchical societies with slaves and serfs, the gods higher up the food chain have to be appeased with sacrifices; in communities where co-operation is needed to survive, you pray to gods asking for their help; in warlike nations you need warlike gods who will be on your side in a fight, and so on. How we interact with our gods reflects how we interact with each other – hence the variety of gods and demons throughout history.

Yet despite the range of gods on offer they have one aspect in common – gods always hold the power, humans, the vulnerability. The defining attribute of a god is that they are immortal and cannot die, whereas we humans are mortal and can be mortally wounded. Vulnerable literally means able to be wounded, and whatever may be the particular powers and attributes of a god or goddess, he or she always has the power to end our lives. A god who cannot kill us is not a god. Death is, therefore, at the heart of every encounter with a God.

A society's gods are personifications of the forces of existence to which we are vulnerable. By praying to them, making sacrifices, doing various deals with them, we hope to gain influence over events that affected our lives yet over which we have no direct control. A society's gods therefore represent the powers and forces that have yet to be claimed by that culture and society. Yet our relationship with the divine is changing.

In our modern world, we are all gods now. We can fly anywhere in the world. We can demand many things as our 'right'. We can release the furies in the heart of the atom. We can fly through the heavens and land on the moon. We hold worlds in the palms of our hands. We can see events as they happen on the other side of the globe. One by one we have persuaded the gods down from Mount Olympus and they have lost their aloofness. The immortal ones have become mortal and now the gods die like men.

We have become the gods we once projected up to the stars because we were not ready to know them for who they really are. The gods are us. We became the creatures of the gods we created until step by step we brought what we had projected skywards back down to Earth. The gods came to Earth one by one, not to save us, to become us.

But if we have claimed many of the powers that were once the province solely of the gods, and we have become the gods we once worshipped, who or what are our gods and demons now?

There is one god left standing. However much we seek invulnerability and equality with the gods through the power and might of our sciences and technologies, there is one aspect of life we do not have power over – death. Aeschylus, the father of tragedy, wrote around 500 BC, 'Of all the Gods, only Death craves neither gifts nor sacrifice, nor offerings; he has no altars nor is he soothed by hymns of praise. He alone, out of all the powers of heaven, is aloof from all persuasion.' Only death now remains like a god – aloof, alone, absolute and immortal.

We may have powers and possibilities beyond the wildest dreams of earlier generations yet, however much power we have accumulated in life, death will always claim us in the end. The inevitable reality of death ensures that we can never truly escape our human destiny and its vulnerable mortality. Death is the last God.

Death is the final frontier. For humanity to expand its consciousness to its ultimate collective fulfilment, which involves knowing the full reality of who and what we are, we have to penetrate the secrets of death. Death holds the keys to the sacred knowledge that we need, perhaps now more than ever before because, paradoxically, the more we have become like gods, the more we fear death. Death is now the only thing left that confronts us with our humanity – that one day we will die. And a society that loses it humanity loses its soul.

Death is the guardian of the sacred in our modern world. This is why a modern narrative of death is so important and why we cannot rely only on the myths and narratives that spoke to our ancestors. Because they lived in a world where the gods still existed; in our post-modern world, God is dead.

Our modern gods are no longer the annihilating forces that could kill us on a whim; they are in Hollywood, on the news, sitting in boardrooms, banks and research labs all over the world. We have become the gods we once feared. Except for the God of Death. The God of Death now holds all the fear that used to be projected on to a pantheon of gods, an array of forces and energies that we could not control. As a result we are more terrified of death than ever before. This is why, in our secular society, we need new narratives of the sacred, ones that will help us encounter our last God with consciousness and love rather than ignorance and fear. And a death that is encountered with consciousness and love is not the annihilation we fear. Death too can become us.

Conflicting thoughts and feelings about Tim's death had been struggling within me for months. We could connect and communicate – we had lost each other forever. He lived on in everyone who loved him – he did not live on, he had died. His spirit lived on in another realm, a different dimension that interpenetrated this one – he was absolutely dead, in all directions, gone. I had another vivid dream.

I meet Tim. He is strong, tanned, healthy, and laughing. I burst into tears and hug him, though I am also laughing because I am so happy to meet him like this, even when I know he is dead. I say – 'I love you so much!' He laughs and we joke, nudging each other, meaninglessly playing and messing around together. Suddenly he stops and says, 'I have missed you.' I know that he means all of us – me, Jo, John, Martin, Chris, Nabil and all his friends. And it is true, everyone he has ever loved is still alive.

'But how can you miss us? You are dead. The dead don't 'miss' the living surely? Aren't you at one with everything and all that?'

'Ah,' he smiles, 'it all can be.'

He puts his arm around my shoulders and turns me round to face a cosmic unfolding in which I can see that while everything changes in time, nothing is lost, and while everything is lost in time, nothing changes. The complete absence of Tim, the oneness with the source, the absolute utter finality of death, the continuation of life in another form, the inconsolable loss, the creative play that continues, the connection that has gone forever in one form but is eternal in another, the mysterious nature of both life and death and their interwoven entanglement, I see that everything is as real as anything else. All of it is what it is. The dimension of time does not allow opposing realities to co-exist in the same place at the same time but, outside the dimensions of space and time, it all co-exists with no problem.

I begin to see that the resolution is not in a particular state but in the flow through them all. I can have Tim with me sometimes, as I did not long after he died, and sometimes there will be only an aching absence. At times I will sense a unique tim-ness in existence forever, at other times a vast empty sky of nothing.

Tim laughs.

'That's it, Mum. On Mondays and Thursdays you can serenely contemplate the transcendental, on Tuesdays and Thursdays, wear black and mourn your loss.' He grins. 'Though your timetable will be ignored; these things happen in their time not yours. Just as my death also happened in its time, not mine.'

We link arms and begin to walk across an invisible path through the darkness of space, gazing at the galaxies and giant molecular clouds all around us.

'You know, Mum, I died so suddenly and so young that I have a lot of un-lived life to get through. I was not old, feeble and grey haired like you, just about managing to stagger across the room to make a chamomile tea.'

I punch him on his spiritual arm. 'I'd have you know I do not stagger, I stride. And I've been known to drink stronger beverages than herb teas.'

He laughs. 'Though admit it – you couldn't have done what I did. I went out blazing. And all that energy does not just disappear; it is transformed. Look over there.' He pointed across the dark night of space to a group of stars pulsating. 'That is a collective of young people who died in wars. They are using their un-lived life to try and raise people's awareness of the stupidity and futility of war. And that crew over there,' he points to a swirling cloud of cosmic dust. 'That's a healing massive. You know all the psychotherapy and healing stuff you're so keen on, well it wouldn't work without the cosmic input of that lot.'

'What about you? I dread to think what cosmic input you are up to.'

'Oh I'm having fun. I've joined a creative crew who inspire musicians and give writers insights. But we've got no ego, remember, so it doesn't bother us that no one knows what we're doing. That's part of

the fun anyway.' He grins. 'But because you are not as ego-less or as wise as me, Mum, I have decided to spend some of my un-lived energy helping you get through my death. I will visit you in your dreams and meditations and we will go on a journey into death together. And you know me, always an eye on the main man – this will help me too.'

'Oh so you need your old staggering mother's wisdom after all.'

'Not as much as you need mine, Mum. I'm not weeping through a box of tissues on a daily basis!'

'Well, you would if it had been me that suddenly died!'

'Ah, but you didn't, I did. And in that is a world of difference. **The** world in fact. Besides, my death is not what it seems.'

He smiles, hugs me and flies off as a comet across the darkness of space, leaving a trail of light rather like his life has left a trail of tim-ness.

Though he has not left me bereft this time because we are going to help each other through and into death. Even if it is only in my dreams.

I woke and opened a book at random from the pile growing by my bed. It was by Elisabeth Kübler-Ross. I read: 'Watching a peaceful death of a human being reminds us of a falling star; one of a million lights in a vast sky that flares up for a brief moment only to disappear into the endless night forever.' But after that dream I knew Tim would disappear only when our job together was done – and that would take longer than a brief moment. Though what is a moment in an is-ness outside time anyway?

We create our own myths and we create out own gods. And although we do not create everything that happens as many New Age gurus seem to tell us, which is a kind of omnipotent fantasy, it *is* up to us what realities we engage and experience, and what we turn away from and deny. And in this way we create ourselves. Perhaps it is even up to us to create our own soul. Gurdjieff, a spiritual teacher in the first half of the 20th century, said we do not automatically have a soul; we are each respon-sible for growing one.

Ideas of the soul have changed throughout history and are as

varied as the cultures that gave rise to them. Many of our traditional Western ideas have their roots in Judaeo-Christian and
Greek ideas, that each of us has a soul, a unique essence that is a
spark of the divine. According to this tradition, the soul is part of
a person's life and on death it leaves the body, taking with it the
memory and wisdom of what has been learned while on Earth.
On death we go through some kind of judgment and re-
education, often with painful realisations about our mistakes on
Earth, until we are ready to enter the bliss of union with God.
Unless we are beyond redemption, in which case we are exiled
from God to one of the graphic hells humanity has imagined.
Some say the purgatorial cleansing is life on Earth – here is the
hell not there. As Tupac Shakur said: 'My only fear of death is
reincarnation.' But most locate the heavenly paradise and its
opposite in another non-material realm.

There is much disagreement about the details but the
monotheistic religions of the Judaeo-Christian-Islamic traditions
pretty much concur that we have one life and one soul, perhaps a
reflection of their one God. Hinduism, on the other hand, has a
multitude of deities and demons, and each soul has multiple
reincarnations. In the Hindu tradition, a human being has no
permanent self; like the rest of nature we live in a continuous
cycle of life, death and rebirth. The soul, the Atman, is not
unique; it is universal and impersonal, present in all living
things, humans, animals, plants, gods and demons. It is part of
Brahman, the godliness of existence. Each soul can achieve
enlightenment through thousands of lifetimes and then returns
to Brahman with no more reincarnations.

In Buddhism all sentient beings have souls and on death these
dissolve back into the consciousness that permeates everything
yet has no beginning and no end. The soul is then reincarnated in
another living form, which may be another human or an animal.
The enlightenment that releases you from the cycle of birth and
death is described within Buddhism as a state of consciousness in

which one has emptied the mind so that it is filled only with the eternal. In this emptiness lie the great freedom of Moksha and the bliss of Nirvana.

A particular branch of Buddhism has evolved in Tibet that pays great attention to what happens when we die. The *Bardo Thodol, The Tibetan Book of the Dead,* was written in the 8th century and clearly describes the stages each soul goes through on death. A person is said to have forty-nine days in which they go through various stages of dissolution, by degrees losing their memory, their worldly mind, their energy flow, all sensory information, until they encounter the *stong-pa nyid,* the great empty. This is the actual loss of consciousness before we awake to the eighth and final dissolution in the clear light of death. We remain in this clear light for three days as our 'truth body' is formed. This truth body then goes into the Bardo of death where it encounters various energies and figures such as wrathful demons or compassionate deities. How the 'truth body' relates with this array of energies determines the nature of the next reincarnation. If we meet them without entanglement, we are freed from another rebirth forever.

An even older text is *The Egyptian Book of the Dead,* written around 2300 BC. This consisted of around two hundred spells that helped the soul on its way through various trials in the underworld to be re-united with the body in Paradise, the Field of Reeds. The spells were needed because the journey of death was seen as being as hazardous as life. They ranged from spells to prevent crocodiles devouring you and demons turning you into a beetle, to spells that helped you remember the names of gods so they would look kindly on you. A person would plan their funeral and choose the spells they thought most useful, which were then written down and placed in the coffin or inscribed on the walls of the tomb. Though the worldly penetrated the celestial, as is the way of things everywhere, and the wealthier you were, the more spells you could afford.

In the Chinese tradition the soul also goes on a journey after death, though every person has two souls, the hun and the po, and they go in different directions. The Hun goes to heaven and joins the ancestors, the Po stays with the body or enters the underworld. Taoist teaching expands on this and holds that a person has ten souls, three hun and seven po. Multiple souls are found in other places too.

Australian aborigines also believe that a person has two souls. One is linked to the particular person and hangs around the living after death until it fades away; another soul returns to the Dreaming and empowers the totemic forces that guide the living. Animals, plants, mountains, rivers, trees and places are all infused with spirit and have souls. Even directions have souls.

Many Native Americans also believe in a multi-dimensional soul, each person having one that departs for the next world and another that remains on Earth, often causing trouble for the living. Though the Navajo have a variety of contradictory ideas of a soul: the soul is unique and eternal, the soul is washed clean of all personality and reborn, the soul does not exist and there is no afterlife, the only immortality being through your descendants.

Indigenous beliefs are not as fixed as the dogmatic doctrines of more organised religions, yet indigenous spirituality always involves the spirit world interwoven with the material world. In these animistic traditions the spirit or soul of plants, animals and places can have dialogues with the human soul, mediated by a shaman. On death a person's soul is said to enter the spirit world, from where it can communicate and work with the living, wait to be reborn, or just to dissolve into the mystery of it all.

Ideas of the soul are complex, contradictory and as different as the cultures that gave rise to these beliefs. A narrative of the soul and the sacred that speaks meaningfully to us in our modern world cannot therefore be simply what spoke to nomadic societies, mediaeval hierarchies, ancient Eastern culture or aboriginal tribes; it needs to reflect the way we live now.

In one of my vivid dreams Tim arrives dressed in his Paul Smith suit and even a tie.

I am overjoyed to see him and we hug; though I also weep because he is dead. He takes me by the hand and we walk towards a presence of tremendous love and light. My sorrow leaves me and I am filled with a joy and peace beyond words. This is where I have come from, where I belong, a home I have forgotten, and I can only describe this as being in the presence of God.

I think of the near death experiences I've read that describe similar experiences – perhaps I am experiencing the part of me that died with Tim. Though if this is heaven, it is not the celestial purity I imagined as a child, with a cathedral like splendour and a God to adore in awe. Tim is joking and messing about with this God-like presence and having fun with irreverent laughter. I suppose the folk who more usually describe such realms tend to be pious types, whereas a party hard north-London lad like Tim is not going to suddenly transform into a being of silent serenity or an angel of sweetness and light just because he is dead.

'No way!' agrees Tim, though I haven't spoken. 'I'll leave all that psycho-spiritual healing gear to you and your friends. You lot can get into the silent serenity of meditation all you like, I'd rather chill with my mates, kick up some fun and party.'

God as a mate to party with – that's not a take I've come across before.

Suddenly I realise that heaven is quite simply composed of every-thing we have ever loved, not what we have liked, wanted, desired, fancied or lusted after, more what we have truly loved and, therefore, have been willing to give our life to. Whatever we are willing to die for, that is what our heaven will be. If we give ourselves to freedom, love or consciousness then these energies will permeate our heaven. If we have truly loved a person, a species of creature, a community, an ideal, then we live on in an eternal interconnectedness with that. Or if our love was for art, music or beauty in some form, then we will live on in the vibrations of those energies forever. Though this also means that if we

*have been willing to die for nothing, because our survival has been the
only sacred object with value and meaning above all else, then that is
what our heaven will be – nothing. We create heaven with our love, just
as we create hell with our fear.*

*Which explains why I am laughing and having fun in this heaven,
joking and playing with this powerful presence of light rather than
blissfully sitting in a silent serenity or falling down in adoration. Tim
gave his all to love, play, creativity, enquiry, music, dance and laughter;
that is what he died for. And this is the realm Tim now inhabits.*

*Tim laughs. 'Yes, you're breaking it down, Mum, yeah, you're
breaking it down.'*

After that dream I began to allow the full reality of Tim's
death, in all its dimensions, even when it veered off into weird
territory with cosmic stardust influencing musicians and anti-
war protestors. And if voices in my head told me that I was
delusional and hiding from the dreadful finality of death with
elaborate fantasises, I would reply: 'On the contrary, I am
embracing a greater reality than the intellectual mind can
tolerate. I am expanding into the extended mind where multiple
dimensions of reality co-exist and where the dead and the living
are codependent creators of love and consciousness.' Or
something like that.

I was reconnecting with Tim in these dreams whatever
explanatory paradigm I might use to describe it. And I was going
to stay on message. Though whether the key thing was the
message, the medium of the message or the meaning of the
medium of the message, I had no idea. Just as I did not know
which was the most significant, the dream, the dreamer or the
interpretation of the dream. And as Chuang Tzu asked – who is
dreaming anyway, do we dream the dream, or does the dream
dream us?

I began to explore contemporary ideas of the soul and life
after death.

5

A Deeper Shade of Soul

It is often said that before you die your life passes before your eyes.
It's true. It's called living.
Terry Pratchett

Contemporary thought on the soul involves several strands. There are the psychodynamic and archetypal understandings developed by Carl Jung, Laurens van der Post, Joseph Campbell, James Hillman, among many others. There is Linguistic Philosophy and its analysis of the nature of meaning and what we can and cannot think about. There are the scientific understandings of modern quantum and astrophysics. And there are the New Age ideas, a spirituality with no confining dogma which uses ideas from traditions all over the world.

The psychodynamic and archetypal approach sees the human psyche as having two distinct aspects, and differentiates between the *spirit* and the *soul*. The spirit is associated with an afterlife in another realm of existence and connected with transpersonal issues. The soul struggles with the suffering of human life and its inevitable anguish and heartbreak. Most religious faith has focused on the spirit and neglected the soul; this approach brings focus back to the soul and its efforts to encounter and learn from the darkness of our human condition.

From this perspective the soul reveals itself through dreams, archetypes and myths, and we need to learn from these because the source of understanding, wisdom and love is not a disembodied existence from another dimension, the source is life on Earth, in a body, with all the conflict and struggle that involves. Life is what gives meaning to it all; the sacred is here not elsewhere. Our soul and our humanity are therefore inextricably linked. James Hillman, the founder of archetypal psychology, writes, 'the soul is what makes meaning possible, deepens events into experiences, is communicated in love, and has a special relationship with death.' Which means the one that dies is the one that matters, because death is at the heart of the sacred.

This approach claims that, without the soul, the spirit is nothing but an ephemeral concept with no meaning. Incarnation is the root of the transcendental not the other way round. Wisdom arrives through our struggles not our serenity. The challenges of life in a body, that require us to kill in order to live, lead to an inextricable predicament in which we are forced to find something other that the fight for survival to give our lives meaning. For other animals it is enough to stay alive because they are unaware of the finality of death. We humans, however, know that death is final. We therefore have to find a dimension that gives the endless fight for survival meaning. Unlike other animals our knowledge of death loads life with almost unbearable meaning. But we need to find that meaning in life, not in the afterlife.

The fulfilment of a soul in death is to be found in the way the person lived their life. Did we create enough love, wisdom, beauty, truth, whatever was our thing, while we were alive so that our legacy lives on in some form? Or did we fail to reach for anything beyond our own desires and survival? In other words, is one's life greater than one's death? That is the question – one of them anyway.

Linguistic philosophy would challenge both the question and its answer. This strand of modern thinking would say we cannot ascribe meaning to such questions as 'What is a soul?' or 'What is death?' because we are being tricked by the nature of language into thinking we are talking about an object which does not exist in that form. We have to either reform our language or under-stand the nature of language itself. A major proponent of this philosophical tradition was Wittgenstein. He wrote: 'There are, indeed, things that cannot be put into words. They make themselves manifest. They are what is mystical.' He would say the meanings of many questions about death and the soul are to be found in the person asking the question not in the question itself. For example he wrote: 'To believe in a God means to see that the facts of the world are not the end of the matter. To believe in God means to see that life has a meaning.' In other words the meaning of the idea of God is to express meaning itself, not the actual existence of an entity we name God. He also wrote: 'If we were to think more deeply about death, then it would be truly strange if, in doing so, we did not encounter new images, new linguistic fields.'

Wittgenstein's Tractatus Logico-Philosophicus was his ambitious project to identify the relationship between language and reality. His last sentence is: 'Whereof one cannot speak, thereof one must be silent.' And it is the case that questions such as, 'What is death?', 'Is there a soul?', 'What happens when we die?', have some of their most profound answers in a silence beyond words. Perhaps this is why communities all over the world honour their dead in silence – because what has happened is greater than anything that can be said. Reality can never be put into words anyway; and there is nothing more real than death. As T S Eliot wrote: 'The communication of the dead is tongued with fire beyond the language of the living.'

A few weeks after Tim had died, I walked along the cliff tops between Whitehaven and St Bees. A narrow path climbed to the top of the headland through bracken, butterflies and the banks of forget-me-nots, foxgloves, red clover and cow parsley. These red sandstone cliffs are home to thousands of razorbills, kittiwakes, fulmars, gulls and colonies of many species of cliff-nesting seabirds, even peregrine falcons, ravens and wheatears can sometimes be seen flying over the sea before veering back towards the fields. I climbed off the path down to where I could be alone with just the birds, lay back, closed my eyes.

Suddenly Tim is with me. I ask him, 'What happened to you, Tim?'
He tells me he felt so ill through drinking after six months off it that he
had smoked some opium to relax and go to sleep until the hangover was
gone, but he was so drunk he didn't know what he was doing.

'When I realised I was dead, it was a terrible shock. The darkness*
was darker than I had ever imagined possible. It was the total blackness
of being blind with no eyes that would ever see anything again. For two
days I lived in absolute night where everything that mattered to me was
lost. The only thing left had been love.'

I can imagine it because I was with him. I also had two days of being
under the ground in an utter and absolute darkness in which nothing
could happen. Life, laughter, Tim, his body, his mind, his self, they were
all gone from me; and even more totally, they were gone from him.

'Everyone I have ever loved and who loved me was left behind. You*
were all alive while I was dead. There was no life flashing in front of me,
no light at the end of a tunnel, no light beings or any of that stuff, just
darkness and death. I visited you, Jo, John, Martin and others, and felt
connected with you through love, then I fell into a kind of limbo. It was
peaceful but with the silence of the tomb. I didn't know where else to go
so I hung around my dead body and waited. And then you came. You
told me that everyone who loved me had become my body in the world
and I was now a free spirit. Suddenly I knew it was okay to be dead. I
had thought death was absolutely the worst thing that could have
happened to me, yet what you said freed me. And it is wonderful. To be
dead is nothing like I thought it would be. It is absolutely amazing.'

'What about reviewing your life, learning from your mistakes,*
seeing where you went wrong?' I ask. 'Doing battle with demons and
deities as you go through the bardos, having your heart weighed in the
balance or whatever?' I am also thinking, 'and seeing how much grief
you have given your mother.'

But death is as remorseless with the living as with the dead.

'No. None of that. For me there were just the two days of death and*
then I took off. I'm having a great time. Though I should say, a great

outside-time, because although time exists in me, I am no longer in time. Just as I used to be in the situation, now the situation is in me. Just as you and I were once in each other's lives and now our lives are in each other. I used to play the field, now the field plays me.' He laughs and spins around. 'And you can't blame me for the nonsense I speak because the words are yours, I haven't any.' He smiles at me. I do not smile back.

'OK, Mum, I can see what a devastation this has been for you, which is why I am here, to help you from another realm. Whenever you need me, just give me a call. Though you'll be fine, Mum. For me of course you already are.'

'Am I asleep? Is this a dream? Are you real or a figment of my imagination? Are you a part of me who is you or a part of you who is me? Or what?'

'Ah this is tricky, Mum. That question is from your intellectual mind and your mind uses language and asks questions in a particular way, yet our connection is not through the mind. Thought belongs to life in the human body, and with no body there is no 'standing-under', and therefore no understanding of, anything. You can speak and understand stuff because you are still part of the world of things, a part, apart, not yet the whole. While I have become it.' He grins. 'I am it all, a dream, real, a figment of your imagination, your son and not your son, a potentiality and an actuality that vibrates in and out of existence continually. I am a blackbird singing in the dead of night. I am the happiness of a warm gun. I am you and you are me and we are all together.' He starts to dance to a hip-hop beat. 'Let me give you a subliminal homily though, happily, a familiar anomaly – the words are not the myth nor the narrative, and cause-effect, not a categorical imperative. 'Cos things are not what they seem to your eyes, but then neither are they otherwise.' He laughs, spins around and dances over the horizon. 'Cos I know, Mum, that in the end, your soul is your best friend.'

The last thing I hear in the distance is his laughter.

I sat up, rubbed my eyes and stared out to sea. A sea mist had dissolved the boundary between sea and sky and there was no horizon. I looked down the sheer cliff. Seabirds called to the wind as they flew beneath me. A cloud, in the shape of a fish, drifted by overhead. Death is either way beyond me, or there is a simplicity here I had yet to grasp. I must do more research. My pile of books on death grew higher.

Once we understand that the language of the sacred is myth, then we can ask questions such as 'What is death?' without expecting an objective answer. Joseph Campbell wrote: 'Every religion is true one way or another. It is true when understood metaphorically. But when it gets stuck in its own metaphors, interpreting them as facts, then you are in trouble.' And not only religions fall into this error. One of Wittgenstein's repeated claims was that science, which makes claims to deal only in facts, has as superstitious a belief system as any religion. He wrote, 'Superstition is the belief in the causal nexus.' Yet the causal nexus, that event A causes event B, is the dominant explanatory paradigm of our culture and the foundation of empirical science. Wittgenstein also wrote, 'Man has to awaken to wonder – and so perhaps do peoples. Science is a way of sending him to sleep again.' But Wittgenstein was born in 1889 and modern ideas of relativity and quantum and astrophysics have challenged the earlier mechanistic Newtonian view of the cosmos. Does modern science have anything useful to say about death?

Traditional empirical science assumes that the material world of separate objects and their interactions, the events we can measure and describe, is the only reality; other dimensions than the material exist only in our imagination. Knowledge is seen as involving only the objective facts of a situation; myth and metaphor are superstitious beliefs or ignorant fallacies. Modern developments in science challenge this materialist dogma, especially the ideas to emerge in modern mathematics and theoretical physics. For example, the concept of quantum entanglement is an attempt to explain how two particles, once they have met, remain forever afterwards connected. This connection transcends time and space so even when they are light years apart, if something happens to one particle, it registers with the other. And if this happens for subatomic particles, what might this mean for us when a person we have loved dies?

Do we perhaps remain connected with dead loved ones through the same overarching transcendentally interconnected energy field? Is this quantum entanglement the equivalent of a love that never dies? When death takes us out of the world of space and time do we enter the subatomic world of vibrating strings and dark energy that breaks out of the constraints of the four dimensions of matter in space and time? Perhaps science can become the source of a new language that can speak of death.

Many theories have arisen to explain the strange behaviour of quantum events and observations of deep space, for example, the fluctuating quantum energy field, the omni-centric nature of our universe, the curved nature of time, the continuous creation of matter in the deep vacuum of space, that matter is not a substance but a string vibrating in ten dimensions, that our universe is just one event among an infinity of events, and so on. A discussion of these is beyond my capacity with only A-levels in physics and maths from a time before even 'black holes' had been conceived. Even physicists themselves have trouble outside their own sphere. Many theoretical physicists acknowledge that few people can understand their latest theories; and even those who do, argue.

Yet even if we do not understand the maths, what these ideas can do is give us ground on which to stand while exploring and developing our own myths of death. Then, if the hard certainties of material empiricism dismiss us as fantasists, we can quote Wittgenstein and point to 'dark flow', black holes and the Zero Point energy field, and carry on regardless.

My own pet theory, with neither research nor equations of

any kind to back it up, is that death can be described as the event horizon of a black hole beyond which we cannot see what happens, but that doesn't mean it is not happening. It has been suggested that black holes are portals into a parallel universe anyway. Not only that but each galaxy is constellated around a black hole. Our own Milky Way galaxy, for example, has a super-massive black hole at its centre, and eventually every one of the Milky Way's vast array of stars and planets will disappear into this black hole never to emerge. Like all human culture and myth is constellated around death, and one day all of this, and each one of us, will disappear into that death never to emerge.

I also like the idea that the dead are the dark energy of the universe. Dark energy cannot be sensed, seen or measured yet without it, the structure of existence would fall apart. Rather like the community of the dead cannot be seen or sensed yet without it the structures of families and society would fall apart. (Interestingly there are two contradictory theories about dark energy. One theory is that it is an intrinsic, fundamental energy of a volume of space – a cosmological constant, an is-ness. Other models, such as 'quintessence', proposes that dark energy is more dynamic and can vary, with different theories describing this differently. If you think about it, rather like theories about what happens when we die.)

It is up to you whether you conclude I am speaking in metaphor or fact. Just as it is up to you to decide whether it matters either way. After all, writing new narratives and myths of death is about something far more important than being right.

The New Age is the name given to an eclectic mix of psycho-spiritual enquiry and process that includes elements from many spiritual traditions ranging from monotheism to pantheism, archaeoastronomy to astrology, ecology to feminism, self-help psychology to shamanism. It took off in the '60s when sex, drugs and rock & roll released the energies of thousands of young people who did not have to march to the drums of war and so could dance to a different beat and make love not war, travel the world, not to kill people or exploit them, to learn from other cultures and question everything afresh. And with the new pill and birth control, a whole generation of women for the first time could enjoy sex and as well as freedom. It was a movement with a creative spirit that revolutionized modern culture. And it gave birth to a spirituality that honoured the body, the heart, the mind and the soul – laughter and spirituality, sex and superconsciousness, love and freedom.

I was part of this river. In the sixties I began my search for freedom, love, the Self, God, enlightenment, consciousness… the name of what I was seeking kept changing, but the search itself did not. I demonstrated against the Vietnam War, joined the antipsychiatry movement, took LSD to open my third eye. I went to the first Women's Liberation Conference in Oxford. I sat in consciousness raising groups, encounter groups and endless meetings in various Marxist-feminist-libertarian-anarchic-neo-Reichian communes in which we decided we needed another meeting to decide whatever we had not managed to decide in this one. I went to India to explore the wisdom of the East and ended up in the ashram of Osho Rajneesh, where I stayed for many years. My journey did not end there; it continued. My book, *In the Dark and Still Moving*, tells the story of my quest, and Tim's book, *My Life in Orange*, tells his story, of the trials and wonders of having been a child of a mother on such a quest.

When Tim was writing his book, we had long conversations about our life together. We tried to fathom why so many intelligent, healthy, privileged people would want to abandon the West and go live in a hut in India and follow a guru. We explored the hidden reasons behind my search for freedom, God, love, enlightenment, truth… We sat in cafes and restaurants, his recorder on, his notebook filling with notes as we argued and discussed our relationship, our lives, the politics of experience, the dialectics of consciousness, the nature of meaning. And why did I run from the ordinary into the extraordinary? What was I escaping? He knew what he had been looking for – me – but what had I been looking for?

When Tim was a teenager we had explored the unresolved pain my search had caused him and our connection and love had deepened as a result. When he was writing his book as a young man, we explored the psycho-political terrain of our journey, the nature of a collective dream, the meaning of religion, the perennial quest for a 'better world'. We compared my generation's challenges and his. We unearthed history to explain the present. We reached new levels of mutual understanding and arrived at fresh insights into the challenge that confronts each generation, to find new forms for old dreams. We had always enjoyed our explorations together. Then came his death and they ended forever.

Once we had walked around Ennerdale Lake. Tim had just been told there was a Hollywood bidding war for *Second Lives*, his book on virtual realities. Robert De Niro was trying to get his phone number to speak with him personally. So was Brad Pitt. His agent had told him, 'On no account speak with these guys! They are like gods. They will dazzle and charm you, and you will say things only to find you have agreed to something that is not necessarily in your best interest. Let me handle it.'

'Of course it might come to nothing,' he had said, as we scrambled over the scree where the footpath seemed to peter out. 'Then again, it could be amazing.'

We had wondered how it had happened that he could end up brushing shoulders with such gods. How strange, how wonderful, how utterly unexpected! Especially when we looked back at our turbulent history.

'Perhaps the real test,' I had said, as we made our way back down to the lakeside arm in arm and I fell into a philosophical mode, 'is not how much we lost or what we suffered on a path we have chosen, it is whether, knowing this, we would walk that same path again.' We had both decided, no doubt about it, we would. But Tim's death changed everything.

For several years after his death I wished I had taken almost every step in the opposite direction – stayed at home and baked apple pie, lived in one house, worked in a steady job, retired on a hefty pension, enjoying grandchildren while reflecting on what a success my life had been and how well I had managed everything. Who wants freedom, autonomy, self-exploration, travels around the globe, adventures into the far reaches of human consciousness, when the price is so much regret you would rather not have done any of it? Yet this was not the whole story.

In my dreams a different scenario was unfolding. Tim's and my journey together had not ended, not yet anyway. Our explorations were still happening and our relationship was continuing. Joseph Campbell wrote: 'Myths are public dreams, dreams are private myths.' In my dreams with Tim I was beginning to create my myth of death, write a new narrative of the sacred, uncover new understandings of the meaning of it all. Gradually some shapes began to appear out of the dark night of Tim's death.

I began to see that different parts of us die differently. The ego-I is not a singular entity; it is a temporary congregation of many energies and states of being. Just like an atom was once thought to be indivisible and is now known to be a collection of energies and particles, the ego-I is also not a 'thing' but a collection of energies and selves. On death, the ego-I that contained the community of selves dissolves, and the different parts are freed to find their next belonging. A death is like the splitting of the atom, it releases tremendous energy and the various elements scatter.

Some may find their next home in the memories and hearts of people who are still alive. Some parts may dissolve back into the source, God, the cosmos, whatever you wish to name the great

Mystery. Some parts may remain connected with the living as inspiration, guidance in dreams, healing forces and so on. Some parts may enter another configuration of energies and reincarnate in another body. Some parts may become resonances in the morphic-resonant energy fields that shape living reality. Some parts may remain in the web of generational love, without which families would disintegrate. Some parts may fall into the absolute freedom of emptiness. Some parts may be gone forever into the eternal night of oblivion.

There is no singular map of what happens when we die. A few of us may unfold into many of these possibilities, many of us may undergo only a few, and some may dissolve into nothing but the oblivion. It can all happen, none of it can happen, or some of it can happen sometimes. Each death is unique. It all depends on what we did with our lives.

We are writing our own myth of death anyway. What matters to us, our hopes and fears, our relationships, what we give ourselves to, what we do with our freedoms and loves, this is the living myth we create whether we do it consciously or not.

A politician was bitten by a dog. A few days later his doctor told him that the lab tests were positive, that the dog had rabies, and that he too was infected. The politician pulled out a notebook and began writing furiously. 'Now, take it easy,' said the doctor. 'No need to start writing your will at this point. We are going to do all we can to pull you through.' 'Will, hell!' snapped the politician. 'This is a list of the people I am going to bite.'

Life is without meaning, we bring the meaning to it. The meaning of life is whatever we assign to it because being alive is the meaning. Our life is the myth we inhabit, that we make real by living it. And whether we die smiling or bitter, biting or laughing is up to us. As a consequence death is as diverse as the lives that precede it. Which makes what we do here on Earth even more significant.

Death renders our lives almost unbearably meaningful because while alive we are laying down the template for our eternity. Though as Charlotte Perkins Gilman wrote: 'Eternity is not something that begins after you're dead. It is going on all the time. We are in it now.'

6

As Close As Close Can Be

The life of the dead is placed in the memory of the living.
Marcus Tullius Cicero

When someone we love dies, their body has gone; it has been buried, burned or fed to vultures. Their touch, their smiles, their voice, these are gone from the material realm for all time. We will never eat dinner with them again, nor swap presents at Christmas nor pick up the phone and hear their voice. Our separate body will find no comfort anywhere because in all directions he or she has gone. Even when we know our love keeps us connected forever, this loss is inconsolable.

Hakuin was one of the most influential figures of Japanese Zen Buddhism. When his Master Shoju Rojin died Hakuin was found weeping by one of his disciples. The disciple asked, 'But you teach us there is no death, all is one – so why do you weep?' Hakuin replied: 'My consciousness is at one with my beloved Master. But my body weeps because it will never look into his eyes again, never drink tea with him nor hear his laugh ever again. It would be cruel to forbid my body its tears.'

The pain of bereavement forces us to redefine and reconstruct our relationship with the dead person. The dead may have relocated to within us rather than without, to beyond rather than here, but wherever our beliefs locate them – in our hearts, in heaven, under the earth or in the energy fields of existence – our love will seek to form a new relationship with the one who has died, simply because love will always find new ways in which to express itself.

Tim's father and I separated when Tim was two years old but we remained friends. When Tim died, his father was very clear, when you die, that's it, you are gone. He has had a lot more experience of death than I have. His father died when he was four, his mother when he was nine. He went to live with his grandparents; his grandfather died the next year, his grandmother the following year. Then the aunt who took him in died a few years later. When we fell in love, he warned me, 'Everyone I love dies.' A few weeks after Tim's funeral he called me.

'Anne, I have had the weirdest dream about Tim. It was so vivid, not like a dream at all.'

'I know what you mean, I have dreams like that too.'

'I've only had the one. I was standing in front of a brick wall that extended in both directions as far as the eye could see. There was one brick missing and through the hole I could see Tim. I called out to him – "Where are you?" He called back – "I'm here, come and find me!"'

'Was that the end of the dream?' I asked.

'Yes,' he said.

'John, take down that wall, walk to its end, climb over it, smash it, go round it, dismantle it brick by brick – anything. Find Tim again. Even if only in your dreams. He lives on in your heart anyway. Whatever else might or might not be going on.'

'What's the point?' he said. 'Tim is dead. He doesn't exist anymore. Nothing can change that.'

Yes, that was the terrible truth – Tim had died. The awful truth for the parts of me still alive and kicking in this body was that he had gone for good. And as I stared into the great emptiness of death, that absolute loss revealed unequivocally that Tim was gone. As a result, like John, I also had difficulty when people told me authoritatively what happens after death. You go to the light. You have a life review. You understand your karmic destiny and choose your next life. You create your own reality and your death is whatever you want it to be. They didn't know any more than I do what happens after death – anymore than anyone who is still alive knows. Yet neither did I know death is the end. For a start my dreams were potent, vivid and visceral; I could not dismiss them as meaningless and neither did I want to. My dreams were part of my journey into death to find Tim again in a new way. And like my life, this journey was unique. Just as ultimately no one can tell another how to live or how to die, so no one can tell us how we will experience the death of someone we love. We each navigate the dark waters of death differently. As E M Forster wrote: 'Even if there is nothing beyond death, we shall differ in our nothingness.'

I might have dreams in which Tim and I explore death, someone else might hear voices, another might see visions, another may gaze into the emptiness and discover themselves differently, another might find new songs to sing and so on. We live our own life and die our own death. Yet, whatever the form our grief takes, universally the dead are no longer with us in the body.

The dead may be waiting to meet us in another realm, in another place, within or without us, between us or beyond us, but they are not where they were. To find them again we must first let the dead die and completely bury them. This is because we can only re-meet them as they are, not as they were.

One woman I spoke with had kept her daughter's bedroom exactly how it had been on the day she died for seven years. Nothing had been moved or in any way changed from that dreadful day. It was simply too painful for her to let her daughter go into death. She told me, 'But then one day I realised that I had to move on, and so did my daughter. I went in there, opened the windows, cleaned up and gave her clothes away. That night I placed an extra seat at the dinner table and told the family, "We now have a dead daughter who belongs with us in her rightful place – in our lives not in a shrine upstairs." And I began to find her again, as my dead daughter.'

We need to find the dead, not only in death, also in life – else life loses important dimensions of meaning. How and where we find them is up to us.

A few weeks after Tim's death, a friend, Nirvana, called me.

'You may not know this, Anne, but many years ago I used to give readings for people whose loved ones had recently died. I no longer do this but after I had visited you in London, I was going down the escalator into the Tube and suddenly I heard Tim's voice in my ear. He said, "Thank you for visiting my mother." I was shocked as I have not spoken with spirits and they have not contacted me for about twelve years, not since my children were born. This was a complete surprise.'

Nirvana is not an ungrounded flake; she is an experienced and wise counsellor. I was immediately interested in what she had to say. She continued.

'I asked Tim, "Do you mind if I ask you a personal question?" He said, "Sure, go ahead." I asked, "Did you have any choice in the time or manner of your death?" He said, "On a physical level it was a complete and utter shock. I never thought this would ever happen. But on a spirit level, you get dealt a set of cards. You have no choice in the cards themselves, but how you play them is up to you. And an early death was on my cards."'

Tim was a poker player. One of his friends was ranked eighth in the world and must have taught Tim a thing or two; on every holiday he would clean us out. We ended up refusing to play him except for matchsticks. Perhaps Tim had learned to play the cards so skilfully, his fated early death was as painless as anyone could wish for, falling asleep in bed and never waking up. Tim had folded and left the table when everything in his life was going well, when he had achieved fame, fortune, the love of a beautiful woman, happiness and love in his family. One of the basic rules for all gamblers – quit while you're ahead. But Nirvana had more to tell me.

'In my experience when speaking with the spirits of those who have died, most seem to lie low for about six months. It's as if they are going

through some kind of re-education process about being dead and part of the spirit world, and during this time they cannot communicate with us directly, although general information about them may come through intermediaries in the spirit world. But every now and then a few souls are able to communicate immediately. Whenever I have met one of these, they seem to be bright lights surrounded by love. Often I weep when I feel them, there is something so beautiful about them, they touch my heart and make me cry. Tim was one of these. You could say he has become an angel if you like, or a god, that is how it feels to me whenever I encounter one of these rare souls.'

I thought – no way, Tim was far from an angel! But I liked the idea of his being a special being full of light who had hit the skies running.

Nirvana was away for a few days but said that if I wanted, she would tune in on Tim and ask him more questions on her return. 'Oh, yes please!' I told her, ignoring the voices in my head telling me I was merely trying to console the inconsolable. Several days later we spoke.

'Usually when I approach the spirits of people who have died they are eager, even desperate, to speak to me, to relay messages to their loved ones. Tim was not. He could take it or leave it, talking to me that is. I got the strong impression that he is in direct contact with you and does not need me to mediate. I also got the message that he prefers it this way, to communicate with you directly. I went ahead anyway but there was something here that I have not come across before. It was a strange sense that somehow you and he are processing his death together. It's hard to explain. It's as if your grief and his death are somehow the same journey. And there is no need for me in this. You are completely connected already. You just need to trust it.'

What did she mean – 'trust it'? Trust what? I definitely had a sense of Tim telling me he was fine, that all was well and there was nothing to worry about, even when I was overcome with grief. I also had a clear sense that he was with me at times. But I wanted more than this. I wanted to know who was this Tim and what was happening to him. I wanted a dialogue with Tim that would teach me about what happens on death. I wanted to *know* where he was and in what form. I wanted it proved to me that my sense of Tim was somehow real and not all in my own mind.

Though it might have been I just wanted him back.

When the individual body dies and decomposes or is burned, all that was connected with our survival dies too. Our fears, deceits and lies, our arrogance and control, our protective strategies and defence mechanisms, our personal hopes and fears, these all die with the body. Yet we are about more than survival. Our struggles include a search for authenticity, freedom and integrity; we extend beyond purely personal concerns and act with generosity, love and altruism; we create qualities such as laughter, play, creativity, beauty and wisdom. And these qualities live in a multitude of ways – in the hearts and minds of those who loved us, in memories, in the extended mind, in heaven, in transcendental realities beyond space and time, in the living legacies of all who knew us, however we like to describe it. But the dead are no longer persons.

Whatever conflict or struggle we had with them, we now have to resolve within ourselves. Whatever the unfulfilled longing or desire we projected on to them, we now have to seek its resolution within our own heart. We, the living, not the ego-less dead, are responsible for how the dead live with us. We can forget them or we can invite them to live in our hearts. We can consign them to the void of non-being or our lives can become their home. We can turn away and build walls with our grief or we can welcome the dead back into our lives differently. How we journey through death with someone will be as unique and complex as was our relationship with him or her while alive. Death ends a life, but not a relationship. Though the nature of that relationship has to change.

Before I could find Tim again as he is, I had to let go the Tim that was. I had to stare right into the sun that is death without blinking and see that the Tim I knew in the body, with his dimpled smile, his flat cap, and his passion for hip hop and reggae, this Tim is no more. All of that Tim dissolved when his body died. This is the inconsolable loss and irreparable heart-break. Yet each time I let my grief wash over me, the catharsis was healing and I felt the past release me. When I wept over Tim's cold body in the morgue, I sensed my body was beginning to let his body go. I had to let go his body, his mind, his future, my hopes, my future, his birthdays, Christmas, grandchildren... so many things. I had to face that there would be no more summer holidays together, no more conversations over dinner, no more playing poker with him into the night. I deleted his last message to me on my phone, put the last photo of him into the album of his life, gave away the sheepskin boots I had bought him for his birthday and so on and so on, each time this was accompanied by another wave of loss in the longest goodbye of my life. But something else was also happening. When I cried over memories and that there would be no more such times together, I felt I was letting go the past and bringing our love into the present.

Each time I let go an aspect of his life, my love for Tim was released from where it had been held in memories of the past or locked into hopes for the future, and arrived more and more in the present. And this is where I found Tim again. Our new relationship was forged in the present because he is with me only in this here and now, not in time, not in the 3-dimensional space of matter.

Sometimes people visiting me are surprised I have no photos of Tim on display. I did, but they were of the dead Tim and one by one I put them away. Tim might be dead to the world, but he is alive in me. I do not need photos of the past to have Tim with me here and now. Mourning the dead, however, is a long and complex process; one day I may bring all those photos out again. After all, our journey with dead loved ones does not end until we ourselves die. And who knows, even then...

Since writing the above a friend's father, an artist, has painted a portrait of Tim for me. This painting is not of a moment in time that has gone; it has some of the complexity and depth of Tim. This man also lost a son who died young. He understands what cannot be spoken, and that too is in the portrait, which now hangs in the centre of our living room. Tim has his place in our home again.

While we are alive, with or without physical mementos of their lives, the dead live on in us. We are their living legacy. George Eliot wrote: 'Our dead are never dead to us until we have forgotten them.' Yet when people we love die, we *never* forget them. They live in us. They become us. They *are* us. When people say they think every day about someone who has died, they do not mean they consciously apply their thoughts to remembering specific things that happened; they are saying this person lives on in them.

But the dead do not live with us in a projected future or back in the past; they live with us only in the here and now. And to bring all our love to the present we have to first let them completely die. That is where the heartbreak lies.

The terrible and wonderful task of creating a new relationship with the dead lies with the living because the living are still moving, breathing, working, doing; the dead are dead, they simply are. Just as one day we will be too. This task is terrible because it involves staring into the void of death without flinching. It is wonderful because we encounter dimensions of the same mystery that gave birth to us. Though whether we describe death as a journey to heaven where angels lead us into paradise or a dark flight down into oblivion, the living create such myths, the dead simply inhabit them.

The languages and symbols we use in our search for what we have lost, for the transformed connection, for the meaning of death and therefore life, can take many forms. These range from descriptions of spirit worlds, heavens, saints, gods and demons, to memories, projections, internalised objects, and transferences, to quantum energy fields, black holes and dark energy, to inconsolable loss, heartbreak and grief. When Tim died I needed the myths and psycho-spiritual narratives of a range of cultures and traditions to help me. And each supported me in a different way.

For a long time I was obsessed to discover what was real, what was true, until it dawned on me that this is not the issue. What I was seeking was not in the stories and dreams themselves, but in my search, in my struggle, in my heart. I no longer care what beliefs or language a person uses to find again their relationship with a person who has died, that is not the point, the relationship is, the love is. And love never dies. Fear dies, separation dies, desire dies, the ego dies, the individual body dies, but love does not die. Love lives on beyond death. The God of Death can destroy many things, but he is not omnipotent; he cannot destroy love.

When someone we love dies, we all discover, in the end, that love is greater than death. Through the unbearable anguish of loss we let go of the dead as they were in life and come to realise that even death does not break the interconnectedness we have with them. We discover that people, animals, projects, communities, ideals, art, enquiry, justice, whatever we have loved, these all share in our being-ness. And even death does not change this. Death can change many things, but not the interconnected transcendence of love.

Death ends lives but not relationships. Death can be described as a transformation from matter to energy, actuality to potential, time to eternity, form to spirit, doing to being, existence to oblivion... yet however we describe it, although our relationship with the one who dies continues, it has to change. Our connection with the dead is not merely a passive fact; it is a dynamic relationship in which the living can help the dead into their death, just as the dead can help the living with their living.

We can help those we love into the fulfilment of their deaths by opening our hearts and minds and simply letting our love speak to them. We might speak to them aloud, write poetry or have conversations with them in our hearts. The dead help the living by becoming part of who we are, by enriching our being-ness through their presence in our lives, perhaps they visit us in dreams or 'speak' to us through natural phenomena. But whatever we say and however we 'say' it, really we are speaking to each other of our interconnectedness and our love.

When Tim had been dead several months, a strange thought kept coming to me, that I should write a symphony for Tim. This was a crazy idea; I have never composed music in my life. But the thought would not leave me.

I tell Martin, 'I will have to take over one of the bedrooms and set up some kind of music studio with all the gear, link up a MIDI keyboard, learn how to play it, learn the software, set up microphones. It's a crazy idea. What do you think?'

'I've no idea. Why don't you open one of your books and see what it says.'

I had taken to grasping at all kinds of psycho-spiritual straws in my blind groping in the dark and chose a book at random. It was by Osho. I opened it and read, 'A truly creative person will always keep moving into the unknown and find new ways to express themselves. A scientist might write poetry and a psychologist might write music. This keeps their creativity alive.'

'I reckon that's a pretty clear message, don't you?' says Martin.

I remembered too there is an Irish tradition that when someone dies, friends pay the local musician/poet to write a song for him or her. When this song is played, it is said to be the only occasion when angels have the best tunes, better even than the devil. Because when these songs are played, the dead dance too.

OK, I was going to write a Symphony for Tim that will make the dead dance.

A friend is a dog trainer. She told me were her son to die, she would go out and rescue a thousand dogs in his memory. A mother whose four-year-old daughter had died told me that she knitted a blanket of squares, each one dedicated to a particular event in her daughter's life. A father whose son had died of cancer in his teenage years set up a charity for unwanted pets.

'My son loved his tanks full of weird creatures,' he told me, 'so I set up a charity to take care of unwanted unusual pets such as snakes, stick insects and tropical fish. And when I feed them, clean out their cages and tanks or take them to a new home, my son is with me.'

Tim loved music. The last piece he published before he died was in the *Observer Monthly Music Magazine*. It came out a few weeks after his death and the issue was dedicated to Tim. Perhaps Tim would be with me in the music.

He was. I know nothing about dance music yet dance beats kept finding their way among the cellos and flutes. I had to learn my way round Logic, a midi keyboard, Tascam microphones, track stacks, mixers, arrange windows, score editing... Nabil, one of Tim's musician friends, helped me with the software and was on the end of a phone, but I still do not know how I managed it given I was continually reaching for the tissues and weeping. I definitely felt Tim's hand in it all. Or rather not his hand, he had no hand. If you like, I sensed the phenomena of Tim's presence influencing reality through a transcendentally interconnected energy field. Or if you prefer: a tim-ness vibrates beyond the event horizon of the black hole of death yet, in the entanglement of our hyper-connected universe, interacts with the material dimensions of space and time. Or maybe a more psychological take suits you: my accumulated experiences of Tim from birth through to death created a body of memories that I can draw on to re-create the relationship with him that I have lost. Or perhaps you prefer a spiritualized angle: Tim's spirit worked with me from where he inhabited another dimension in a different realm. Feel free to construct your own take on it all. I did. Tim was with me and we wrote a Symphony together.

I have no other explanation for the fact that in nine months I went from complete ignorance to writing a Symphony for Tim that was later released by Cherry Red Records (and can be downloaded on Amazon, iTunes etc). No way could I have done that alone.

When Tim died I made a vow to him that I would take care of his wife – and I did. We are very close. Five years later she is with another lovely man and has a beautiful baby. Tim, my dead son, her dead husband, is part of all our lives, including hers, including her new partner's. Not as the individual he was, more as a form of love. We might personify his presence as a spirit, or an angel, or we might describe this presence as an energy field or vibration, but really we are speaking of our love. Fortunately Jo's new partner understands this and has also opened his heart to me. I had imagined that I would discreetly fade away when her new partner arrived, even more when their baby was born, but they have insisted Martin and I are part of their family. And of course I am delighted to have a beautiful little grandchild given to me. The love has grown through what was the most dreadful loss.

As soon as I heard Tim was dead I knew my old life was over and that I would never get over his death. And I won't. And I don't want to. I had to integrate this devastating loss into my life. It takes a long time to discover that although the person has died, our love and the relationship we had with them does not die – it transforms. Anyone we have loved shares in our being-ness, and we can never lose that. Through our grief we find a new way of being with them in our hearts. But first we have to let them go in the longest goodbye of them all. This is the inconsolable loss. But as Washington Irving wrote: 'There is a sacredness in tears. They speak more eloquently than ten thousand tongues. They are messengers of overwhelming grief... and unspeakable love.' I had to grieve the irreplaceable, irretrievable and inconsolable loss of Tim in its fullness, because only then could I turn around and find him again in a new way, in my heart, in life.

It was years after Tim had died. Tim had dissolved back into the mystery and was resting in peace. Like a comet that had blazed up in a dark sky and lit up the night, the long trail of tim-ness had finally faded and he was back in a one-ness with the source. My vivid dreams had ended. I no longer felt him sit next to me. Even though our love remained, he had gone. It was his birthday, four years after his death. I was heartbroken all over again at the loss of him in the world. That night I had a lone vivid dream.

Martin and I are moving out of a house to go on a journey. We are carrying bags and as we emerge from the basement to leave we have no hands free to turn on the light at the bottom of the stairs. Suddenly Tim's hand stretches over my shoulder and turns on the light for us. I turn in surprise and there he is, smiling, very close to me right on my shoulder. I am utterly delighted to see him. No tears this time just sheer happiness to see him again. And I see in his face the innocent happiness of Tim as a child and the mature wisdom of the man. All of Tim is here. 'And I am as close as close can be,' he tells me.

I wake up and yes, he is as close as close can be.

Where are the dead? They are waiting to be found in our hearts. They are waiting for us in the singing of birds, the wind in the pines and moonlight on water. They visit us in our dreams, flashes of memory and ritual anniversaries. The dead are wherever we are.

When someone we love dies, often we want to die ourselves because we think that is the only way to be with them again. But as long as we are alive we will find them in life, not in death. We meet the dead deep in the here and now, because this is where we all are. Just as they are waiting to meet us in our death when we too will become part of the eternal belonging beyond all duality.

Though that re-meeting is not as you and me, us and them, he and she, it is a vast 'we' beyond even the duality of being and non-being. Which is why first we have to weep the inconsolable tears of those who have lost what they love so much. Then we discover we have not lost the love we had with that person, it is always with us. This love is the great discovery in death. We find the love in which we find ourselves, each other, and all that we have ever loved – though perhaps it is the love that finds us. And in that love we find we are eternally as close as close can be.

7

The Time of Our Lives

Non omnis moriar multaque pars mei vitabit Libitanam – Not all of me will die, the greater part of me will avoid the goddess of death.
Horace

Funeral rites are as old as humanity. Even 300,000 years ago, Neanderthal men and women were buried with some form of ritual; burial sites have been found where skeletons of Neanderthals have layers of pollen over them indicating they were covered in flowers. In some rituals people tear their clothes, fall to the ground, throw themselves over the body, sing out the whining keen of the death wail. Others cover themselves in ash, wear black, sit low in Shiva, conceal their faces. Some cultures and religions put up a permanent memorial, a gravestone, a statue or bury the dead in family mausoleums. Others give the body back to nature. They feed the body to vultures in Tibet. Sikhs scatter the ashes into rivers. In Guinea they throw the body into the sea. Yet whatever the ceremonial rite, the funeral is a final goodbye to the dead body.

But a funeral is for the living as well as the dead, and all cultures have a ritual that honours a death in the coming together of those who knew the dead person. This congregation is itself a living memorial to the one who has died. The body of the person is buried, burned, fed to vultures or thrown to the sea; their body becomes the body of all who loved them.

We, his close family and friends, scattered Tim's ashes on his birthday, on Hampstead Heath, the scene of many of his triumphs and despairs, loves and losses, and then followed this with another ritual Tim would certainly have approved of – a party.

We meet for lunch on the Heath. We toast Tim with champagne and set off on a tour of the sites of Tim's many and varied adventures on this Heath. We pay our respects to the tree root that brought him off his bike at eleven years old and knocked him out. We look up through the old oak tree he and his friends climbed to smoke dope, hidden in its branches when they should have been at school. We visit the pond where we used to swim, the picnic spot where he kissed his first love, the circle of pines, where it is rumoured Boudicca is buried, and where he and his friends took ecstasy and danced all night. We stand on Parliament Hill where we had watched fireworks, slid down on sledges in the snow and seen the skyline of London change through the years.

We have no plan; spontaneously one of us remembers a place and leads the others there. We stand in a line while it is explained what happened here, though I suspect we hear censored versions for some of the territory. Then we dip into the urn, take a handful of Tim's ashes, angel dust according to Majid, and throw the remaining molecules of what had once been Tim's body into the air on his last flight into oblivion.

A strange wind arrives. It is warm and envelops us, unpredictably strong and gusty then just as suddenly a balmy breeze. This unpredictable wind takes the ashes and swirls them into cloud shapes that twirl before they spread through the sky and disappear. This strange wind springs up time and time again just as we throw the ashes.

Passers-by take photos. Children point and stare. 'If I hadn't got used to strange things happening around Tim's death, I would be seriously spooked!' says Nabil. 'As it is, I now know it is just Tim having some fun.' We have photos of the strange shapes of these clouds. I do not even try to explain them; we are in a cloud of unknowing. Soon there is nothing left of Tim's earthly form.

The warm, breathing, moving animal body dies. The terrible loss of death is that the 'soft animal' that is your body has all life gone from it. And when the body dies, all that was inextricably connected with that body also dies.

The defence mechanisms we so painstakingly constructed over many years die. They were put in place to stop us being wounded and killed; once we are dead, there is no more need for them.

Our cognitive logical mind dies. It was part of the neural circuitry that enables us to manoeuvre through life in the material world. On our death we leave that world behind.

Fear dies. All fears can be traced back to a fear of pain, madness or death, but once we are dead none of these can threaten us ever again.

The ego dies. The ego is the personality we have evolved to carry us through the struggles and tribulations of life in a body, and so when we die we no longer need the ego. Our hopes and fears, our desires for power and status, our righteous convictions, our wish to dominate and control, our placating strategies, our distractions, our manipulations, seductions, bullying, posturing, threats and deal making, these all die. Because the whole point of them was to protect us from harm, and once we are dead, we are beyond all harm.

Everything that lives in time dies because death is the end of time. When human beings created time, we were evolving the power to manipulate the future. Though perhaps we did not realise the price to be paid for such magic was death. But not all of us lives in time. As William Morris wrote: 'The past is not dead, it is living in us, and will be alive in the future which we are now helping to make.' Or as William Faulkner wrote: 'The past is never dead. It's not even past.' Yet another paradox: the human mind's creation of time has enabled our survival while bringing us closer to death.

The world is built on time. The business of the world is to thrust forward in a continual progression towards goals in the future, to work towards manifesting whatever is our hope, our vision. Yet when we live in time, things happen sequentially, and therefore death exists. Without time there would be no death; everything would be happening all of the time, everywhere and always. As Osho said, 'Time is the field of death.'

> *A martial arts student went to his teacher.*
>
> *'I am devoted to studying your martial system. How long will it take me to master it,' he asked earnestly.*
>
> *'Ten years,' the teacher replied.*
>
> *'But I want to master it faster than that!' said the student. 'I will work very hard. I will practice everyday, ten or more hours a day if I have to. How long will it take then?'*
>
> *The teacher leaned back in his chair, adjusted the folds in his robe and took a sip of water.*
>
> *'Twenty years,' he said.*

On death we have no more time left because death is the end of time. The parts of us that die are the parts of us that live in the world of time. The world, the future and death are inextricably linked. The death of our hopes feels like the end of the world because in a way it is; it is the end of the world built in time and the beginning of life in the present. Yet when there is no future, and therefore is no world, there is the here and now of life.

Human beings seem to be the only creatures that live in time. The other animals live in the moment in an instinctual simplicity where impulse and action are one; they have not split life into right and wrong as we have, have not divided life in order to rule over it, have not alienated themselves from their natural instincts in order to create culture and civilization. We humans created time when we began to sacrifice the impulse of the moment for a calculated future gain. This gave us great power to conceive possible futures and the capacity to manifest them, but we paid a price. We alienated ourselves from the flow of energy in our bodies and began to live with inner conflict. The first war was the one we declared on ourselves, when we began to live in time rather than the moment.

Yet only an animal divided from itself in time can look back at itself and become consciously aware of its self, its history, its future – and therefore its death. Thus only a self-conscious creature living in time is therefore afraid of death. Other animals do not live in a fear of death. The struggle for survival is the instinctual engine of evolution and so an animal will fight for its life; but it does not fight because it is afraid of death, it fights because it is committed to life.

Other creatures still live in an instinctive Garden of Eden. They are not divided from themselves by morality nor do they have, therefore, any consciousness of death. They live in the moment, outside time. Though, let's be clear, their Eden is a jungle not a lawn with perennial borders – when we take our dogs for a walk, they are not out to enjoy the view; they are on the hunt for creatures to kill and eat. Yet as Ludwig Wittgenstein wrote, 'If we take eternity to mean not infinite temporal duration but timelessness, then eternal life belongs to those who live in the present.' Animals already have eternal life. We have to die for it.

A modern understanding of death requires a modern understanding of the ego, as it is the ego that lives in time and therefore dies. But what is the ego? Many Eastern philosophies would tell us, the ego is something that keeps us imprisoned within delusions and to find true wisdom the ego must die. Freudians would say the ego is the self-awareness that marks us out from the other animals and continually mediates between the super-ego and the id. Jungians might define the ego as the set of inner selves we are aware of and that we think is who we are, whereas in reality we have within us an infinity of possibilities. Psychologists say the ego is the gradual construction of a sense of identity, an 'I', that is created through the relationships a young child develops with those around him or her. 'Ego' has also come to mean an arrogant assumption of superiority, conceit and self-importance. Whether a creative necessity, a destructive prison or a sense of superiority, the ego is a complex creature. And it is an essential aspect of our humanity. It protects us.

The first law of the jungle is 'eat or be eaten'; anything with no protections against being eaten would have become extinct long ago. All living things have therefore evolved ways in which they defend themselves from being killed and made a part of something else. The human animal has aeons of evolution behind it, millennia in which we have learned to survive.

We try to control life to avoid being harmed. We have to. This control is not only needed for survival it is essential to develop the power to create or do anything – even amoebae control what aspects of their environment they will allow through their cell wall and what they keep out. In human beings, unlike most other species, this control can be conscious and deliberate; our tactics therefore can be psychological as well as instinctual and behav-ioural. The patterns of our control and defence constitute our ego.

To the extent we are identified with our survival, we will be identified with our ego – because that is the function of the ego, to ensure our survival. Part of becoming human is to construct an ego that protects us. Yet humans cannot rely on instinctual mechanisms alone because we are social creatures and many threats to our welfare and happiness are social and psycho-logical. So what do we do? We learn to control the way life flows through our body as a way to control our experience. All power in the world has its origin in our control over the energy of our body. Every technique an animal has evolved to protect its survival has an equivalence in our human armoury – fight, flight, hide, disguise, placate, seduce, puff up, play dead, undermine, armour, poison, weave webs, camouflage, hiding in the herd, creating alliances. These instinctual defences are of the body, to protect the body.

As babies we were utterly vulnerable. Everything affected us;

we could be hurt, neglected and abandoned, and there was nothing we could do about it. In order to protect this deep vulnerability, we have to develop some power and control. The first power we discover is over our own bodies. We learn to reach out for things we feel drawn to, and to pull away from things that threaten us. We begin to tense our muscles to prevent our natural spontaneity, and over time patterns of this tension evolve that stop certain feelings or movements while allowing others. Gradually we notice that this control over our own body also influences what happens around us. When we smile or cry we see this affects others, so we learn to use our developing self-control to have a degree of control over first those close to us and, later, the world. These control patterns form our ego.

Eventually our patterns of self-control become so automatic we believe these control patterns are who we are. We think we are tough because we have lost our tender aspects, or that we are tender because we have lost our tough aspects. We think we are independent because we have buried our needs, or that we are helpless because we have buried our self-reliance, and so on. Our personality, our ego, is nothing more than the restricted energy and feeling that we have allowed to flow through our bodies. Really our personality is only the tip of an iceberg; underneath the water, buried in our unconscious, lie energies and potential-ities way beyond who we think we are. But there is a difficulty when we try and connect with these buried parts of ourselves – what is beyond the ego appears threatening, which is why we repressed it in the first place. And so expanding our under-standing of who we are beyond our ego-identity is not easy; it is frightening and involves confronting the very fears that led us to construct those defences in the first place.

On the physical level the ego is the pattern of tension in the body that we each developed to protect and defend ourselves – it is therefore a map of our fear. When we become identified with our ego and survival, we become imprisoned within that fear. To examine what is beyond the ego, and may therefore continue to exist after death in another form or formlessness, involves re-encountering the helpless vulnerability we have spent our lives running from, the same that led us to build a protective ego in the first place.

In the end, we cannot escape this vulnerability anyway. We are as helpless and vulnerable in the face of death as we were as babies in relation to life. And anyway when we die there is nothing left to protect, and so the defences that we have spent a lifetime developing and perfecting die too. We no longer need them.

We no longer need them because when we die we are no longer in control of our experience. We have no more control, power or will over anything, not even ourselves. We happen. We unfold. We are. The more we are identified with our power and control, therefore, the more we will fear death, because death is the surrender of all our power and control.

I have another vivid dream. I am at a table with four people I do not know. We are discussing death and dreams. They agree that death is like dreaming, swirling and insubstantial, seeing vaguely in a half-light. I tell them I have some dreams that are not like that, ones that are vivid, full of colour, with an almost tangible clarity. They try to persuade me I am mistaken, that it is just my imagination. Suddenly Tim is next to me on my right. Ignoring the others completely, he tells me:

'Death is not like that. Do not listen to them, they are talking with just their minds, and the mind can never know death. Only consciousness can know death and that is of our beings not our intellect.' He leans in closer to make sure I listen to him and not to the others. 'When you are alive and dream, only a part of you can dream because the rest is still committed to the body and being alive. You still have to breathe and move, your heart has to beat, your liver and kidneys have to work. But when you are dead, the dreamer is all of you. As a result, the focus and clarity is amazing.' He is intent that I understand

him. *'Being dead is like dreaming in that anything can happen, but death is not a blurred looking through a glass darkly at all, it is vivid, shiny, sharp, potent. I should know – I'm dead.'*

This is not the laughing, playful Tim I have met in my dreams before. He is focused and serious.

'Come with me, Mum, I want to show you something.'

We leave and walk outside into a wood. It is autumn and we walk through mist and layers of dead leaves.

'Look around you, what do you see?'

I see a dead log covered in moss and lichens and watch a beetle climb through its cracks. A vole darts between damp hiding places, a dead spider in its mouth. Above, two squirrels leap from one tree to another, for a moment they are flying. They land and leaves fall.

'I see life,' I told him.

'And me, do you see me?'

'Well yes, you are here beside me. But I know you are dead and this is a dream.'

'But what is a dream? A dream is a journey, a gift from the dream weaver, the royal road to the unconscious – take your pick. I am in your dream and you are in mine. We are dreaming each other. Reality is the dream we have agreed to dream together. Or, if you prefer, reality is the dream that has agreed to dream us.' He links his arm with mine and we walk in silence through the dappled sunlight and the sounds and smells of this wood.

I do not want this dream to end. I want to walk with my son as we have done so often while he was alive. I do not want him to be dead. I have not spoken but he hears me.

'But I am alive in this dream.'

'Yes, but I am going to wake up and you will be gone.' Tears fall down my cheeks.

'Yes, when you wake up, as soon as you open your eyes, the world will be formed all over again. And you are right, you will be dreaming the world and I will not be there. My dream of the world has ended.'

My tears fall down my face and into the earth.

'Let me explain, Mum. The world is built upon a construction of the future, and so of course the dead do not belong in the world anymore. Their time has ended. But the world is not the Earth. I have left the world but not the Earth. It will help you if you understand this, Mum – my time in the world has ended but not my life on Earth.' He gestures to the life in this wood all around us. 'I belong to this. I belong to life because life includes death. I belong to the moment where it all happens, including death. I belong to everyone and everything that I have ever loved. I belong to this dream, just as this dream belongs to us because we are both dreaming it.' He stops and turns me to face him. 'You too, Mum. Your home is no longer the world. You also can only belong to what includes death – because I am your only son and I am dead.'

'Yes it's true, I no longer belong to the world, not as I did anyway.' I wipe my tears and look up through the trees to the sky. I remember all the things that used to matter to me, success, recognition, a fancy home, shopping, parties… all of which are of no importance whatsoever to me now. 'But if the world is not my home, where do I belong?'

'You'll have to answer that, Mum. As for me…' He does a few dance moves and sings, 'I'm everywhere and nowhere baby, that's where I'm at.'

I frown and kick a few dead leaves. 'Perhaps we belong to our love. After all it is because I love you that I left the world and came with you into your death.

'Hey, that's good, we belong to our love. I like it!' He laughs. 'Though don't throw away your tissues yet, Mum – you'll forget all this when you wake up in the morning and find yourself back in the world.' He smiles and dissolves into the trees and the wind, into the rustling of leaves, the songs of the birds and the movements of beetles. He is gone. And he is here.

Many spiritual traditions describe the evolution of our consciousness as a path towards enlightenment, holiness, wisdom, shamanic power, whatever word is used, on which we go through various stages until there is a transition from one level of consciousness to another. Different traditions will describe this transition in different ways, from duality to oneness, darkness to light, imprisonment in fear to liberation from fear, a shift from the vibration of matter to the higher vibration of energy, from struggle to surrender, and so on. Yet whatever the description, all traditions involve an encounter with death. Many spiritual paths describe this in terms such as the dark night of the soul, the end of desire, emptying the mind, surrendering to the will of God. But all agree, there can be no enlightenment without an experience of death, frequently described as the death of the ego.

We have seen how the ego is a collection of our defence mechanisms and is therefore a map of our fear. It can also be described as the persona we adopt to live in the world. The ego is the way we survive in the world of time and space in a body that dies. Ram Dass described the ego as a space-suit; we need it to breathe but it is not who we really are. Elisabeth Kübler-Ross described it as a winter coat that we put away when spring comes. Buddhists might say the ego is attachment to our desires. Yet whatever our metaphors, the death of the ego is said to be a liberation from the prison of our fear. And since all fear has its roots in our fear of death, the death of the ego is the end of our fear of death.

This transition from fear to freedom would perhaps be better described as a dis-identification from our ego rather than the death of the ego. After all we need the protection of that space-suit if we are to operate in the world because however much we might dress it up in designer clothes and charming smiles, the world is a jungle as much as a garden; and in a jungle, every creature is a potential predator we must guard against. Yet the reason it is often called the death of the ego is that as we go beyond our fears, it feels like death.

To move beyond the fear of our ego requires us to encounter and experience the very fears that led us to construct the ego in the first place. And because we have managed to vanquish so many of the gods and forces of existence that we were once vulnerable to, our modern fear tends to be focused almost entirely on death. We no longer expect to face starvation in a drought, or have our whole family die of a plague, or our homes lost in a forest fire or destroyed by termites. We have less fear now for our survival on a daily basis, but a more potent existential fear of oblivion. Whether we are conscious of this or not, this fear drives us. This 'driven-ness' is another way to describe the operation of the ego.

There is a saying: the quickest way to heaven is straight through hell. It is the only way. You cannot go beyond something until you have gone into it. And so death, which takes us beyond all fears, involves an encounter with each and every one of our fears. To move through our ego and its preoccupation with survival therefore feels like death. In a way, it *is* a death. This is exactly what happens on death; we go beyond our fears and on the way we encounter them. Though it is up to us whether we call them hell, the death agony, unresolved conflicts, archetypal fears, wrathful demons, the void or a nightmare.

Kabir was a mystic who lived in India in the 15th century. He combined elements of Hinduism and Islam yet denounced more usual ways to connect with God such as endless chanting, fasting and austerities. He said you had to put aside the Qur'an and the Vedas and learn directly from life. Kabir wrote that when he made the leap from the darkness of his ego to the light that is beyond it, he saw the ocean burning and fire very cold, fishes running on dry land and trees whose roots were in the sky, summer arriving before spring and parents becoming younger than their children. Kabir was describing in symbols the turmoil of consciously extending beyond the ego into the death-less.

When we move beyond our ego, the world as we know it ends, time ends, our assumptions about reality are overturned –

exactly what happens on death. This is why when we extend beyond the ego and move from the world of time and duality into another dimension of reality that is unknown and eternal, it is often called the 'death of the ego', because we go through a death.

Though that death may not be what we fear at all.

A famous warrior visited a Shaolin monk and invited him to a duel.

'Fight me and we will discover which of us is superior. Though I must warn you, I will win.'

'And I should warn you too,' said the monk.

The warrior laughed. 'What you! You are a vegetarian who does nothing but sit about all day meditating! You know nothing of significance!' And he unsheathed his sword.

'But I know about death,' said the monk. And he touched his sword beside him.

The warrior leaped up. 'Be very afraid, monk!' He waved his sword around. 'And get ready to die!'

'I am not afraid,' said the monk. 'And I am always ready.'

The warrior lunged at the monk shouting: 'I am about to cut off your head – you could at least put up a bit of a fight before I kill you!'

'It is already over,' said the monk.

'What are you talking about? We haven't even begun yet!'

'Just nod,' said the monk.

Our fear dies. It was a temporary phenomenon concerned with what might happen in the future, most potently our death. Our defensiveness dies. Our attempts to escape death by escaping life die. Our focus on the future rather than the moment dies. Our will to make life conform to our ideas for it dies. Our preoccupation with how others see us dies. All the attributes of our personality that were concerned with staying alive die. These aspects of our ego live in time; on death there is no more time.

And so all that lived in time dies.

It is possible that our defensiveness and fear do not absolutely die. Perhaps the structure of the ego dies, but the energy of the ego does not. Maybe our preoccupation with money, power and status and our determination to survive whatever it costs, even if it costs the Earth, have to return to Earth to resolve themselves. These aspects are of time, so they cannot find their resolution outside time, in eternity.

Perhaps this recycling of unresolved energies in various reincarnations provides the impetus for life to evolve more love and consciousness. After all that is what so many Eastern spiritual traditions tell us. But even if this is what happens to unresolved elements of our psyche, the particular ego-I that I call me, in this time and place, can never reincarnate. This is inextricably connected with this body, the one that dies, and so dissolves on death completely. It will be in another ego-I in another time, another combination of energies that have temporarily come together and, when the time comes, will also disband.

The spiritual journey involves going beyond the ego or dying to oneself, while still alive. This death in life is not therefore an unconscious process of death that simply happens to us; it is a conscious death of the kind described by Matthew in his Gospel, 'of losing one's life to find it.' Or as Buddha said, 'ultimate freedom is the death that detaches you from all your desires.' Because whether we go through those gates while alive or when we die, death is the gateway into the timelessness of eternity, into the peace that passeth all understanding, into the mystery that lies on the other side of our ego.

In the end, we always transcend the individual ego anyway. Death is the final expansion beyond all selfhood. On death our being and consciousness spread throughout the cosmos. There is no more separate 'I'. The 'I' becomes 'we' and we permeate everything. We become no-thing; we become it all. Including death. As the Chandogya Upanishad, one of the most ancient scriptures in the world, tells us, Tat Tvam Asi – Thou Art That. And whether we die in life, in the afterlife or in another life, at the end of all days, each of us will be here, where nothing exists and everything is. Death reveals that though we exist in time, we belong to eternity.

In the final words of Tilopa, the Indian Master who developed Tantra and whose mystical insights are in the form of his 'Song of Mahamudra': 'The supreme understanding transcends all this and that. In the end it is a great vast ocean where the lights of mother and son merge in one.'

8

In the Blink of an Eye

The past is not dead, it is living in us, and will be alive in the future
which we are now helping to make.
William Morris

Every living body is vulnerable, able to be wounded, and
therefore mortal. Life, as we know it, could not exist otherwise;
the continuation of life depends upon all creatures eventually
dying. Each creature on its death renews and enriches life
through whatever is its legacy. This legacy has many dimensions.
On the physical level our lives are food for more life; we are
molecules endlessly recycled, nourishment for creatures still
living, part of the Body of the goddess Gaia. On cultural and
social levels we leave our imprint in the hearts and minds of all
who knew us, we live on through our children and friends and
we leave legacies of our time on Earth that feed and maintain
society and culture. On the psycho-spiritual level we leave a
legacy of the soul we forged in our struggles to live with
integrity and dignity. Consciousness, love, freedom, beauty,
laughter, whatever we created during our time in a body on
Earth forms our legacy, our gift back to life as we leave. And for
each one of us that legacy will be as unique as was the life that
preceded it.

Some may leave only a physical legacy with their molecular
elements reconstituted in a worm or leaf. Others may have some
quality of their being-ness continue through their children or in
a material legacy such as a building or work of art. Perhaps
something of a life may also live on as an inspirational force, an
idea that has a life of its own, a meme in the cultural zeitgeist. We
might describe our legacy as a resonance in the cosmic ohm, a

reincarnation in a different ego, an eternal spirit, an indefinable element in the eternal mystery, but whatever words we use, the list of potential ways we live on is as diverse and as multifaceted as are our lives. And life is not just the warm animal body.

Life is the continuous unfolding of the great and mysterious event that is this universe. Life is the living, breathing bodies of all creatures great and small, the force fields of the cosmos, dimensions beyond time and space, vibrations that permeate reality yet can neither be named nor known. And as long as there is life, we do not leave our legacy behind – we become it. We live on in life as our legacy.

When Tim had been dead nine months, my vivid dreams stopped for a period. I did not feel him visit me. I no longer heard his voice speaking to me in my mind. Maybe if I meditated more or opened my third eye wider to the Spirit World, I could call him back from the dead again. Or perhaps I simply have to let him go once again in the longest farewell of my life as the wave had finally fallen into the ocean and lost its distinct and unique shape forever. Another wave may be formed with some of the same water, but not that wave. Not my son. Not Tim. Not the person I knew for thirty-four years.

During this fallow period I visited London, where I met up with many of Tim's friends. One of them showed me his leg covered with a full colour tattoo of Tim holding a balloon that had been on the cover of My Life In Orange.

'Anne, look at this, what do you think?'

'My goodness, it's amazing!' I told him. 'That must have hurt.'

'It was agony!' he laughed. 'But when I went walking in the Himalayas to try and get over his death – Tim was literally walking with me all the way.'

Another friend showed me Tim's face on his arm.

'It's brilliant,' he told me. 'Whenever I'm in trouble I touch it and immediately I feel Tim comes to help me.'

Another friend took off his shoe and revealed 'Tim Forever' tattooed

on his foot. Another had a T and a pair of wings on the back of his neck.
'Tim is now behind me all the way,' he grinned.

My vivid dreams had stopped for a while but I found Tim again in the legacies of his life that were still here. And there were many ways in which Tim lived on, in his books, in the hearts of hundreds of people who knew and loved him, in our memories of the adventures we had shared with him, in the gifts he had given us over the years. His legacy was all around us. He was all around us. Though I must admit, to find Tim in tattoos was a bit of a surprise. I doubt my legacy will involve any tattoos, but then one's legacy is as unique as one's life. Tim's legacy lay partly in these tattoos because they were manifestations of the love of his friends and their continuing relationship with him. Tim lived on in our lives, in us in a multitude of ways. He lived on in our love.

But if death is not the end of our essential being-ness, which lives on in our legacy in a multitude of forms, why are we so afraid of it?

When we die we no longer belong to ourselves, we belong to the cosmos. My individual soul and the qualities that made me unique, on death, become no longer 'mine', they become 'ours'. The separate entity who owned things, who laid claim to 'me' and 'mine', no longer exists. It cannot. The individual body that was its source has died. Death annihilates the separate self of the ego and hence the ego is afraid.

The dissolution of the separate self on death is particularly difficult within modern culture because the individual is our most significant identification within society. We pay more attention to the rights of the individual than we do to the responsibilities of community. We hold individuals responsible for their acts, not their families or communities. And, on the whole, we protect and value what is 'mine' more than what is 'ours'. Our modern society is a highly individualised culture with important personal freedoms, without which we would still be serfs or locked into a particular class or caste. No way would we wish to return to the days of slavish acceptance of our place in a preordained order with none of the freedoms previous generations fought for. Yet though we have claimed our individual freedom, we have lost touch with our interdependence. For example we are more aware that we belong to ourselves than that we belong to each other, which is why we can so carelessly destroy what sustains us – our environment, other species and the biodiversity of our ecosystem. Though on death we return to this greater belonging anyway.

Our death involves giving ourselves, and all that we have created, back to life. What was once 'mine' then belongs to the whole. Jean Anouilh wrote: 'Love is, above all, the gift of oneself.' Death can be seen as the ultimate act of love.

The opposite of the expansion of love is the contraction of fear. We could say that we are terrified of death because we do not love each other or life enough, because if we truly love life, when it is time for us to leave, we will give the fruits of our labours while alive back to life with generosity and grace, and possibly even joy. Unfortunately we often die in fear rather than in love, which makes dying far more painful and traumatic than it needs to be. Yet there are far more frightening things than death.

A Sufi story tells of a king who feared wasps and so declared they were abolished. As it happened the wasps didn't listen to the decree, nor did they do any harm to the king. Though the king was eventually stung to death by scorpions.

As Plato warned us long ago: 'Be sure to fear the right things.' And there are far worse things than death. Far worse than death is to live a life in which there has been no love, and therefore no gift back into life when we die. If we have lived concerned only with our own personal survival then, when we die, there is oblivion, because of course, in the end, we do not survive. The real tragedy of life is not death, it is when we sacrifice everything that makes life worth living to live a little longer in a life that is not, therefore, worth living. In which case our legacy may be merely to serve as a warning to others. Martin Luther King said: 'If a man hasn't discovered something that he will die for, he isn't fit to live.' Another fighter of oppression, Ché Guevara, wrote: 'We cannot be sure of having something to live for unless we are willing to die for it.' Both men gave their lives for their visions of freedom. And their legacy lives on. Their legacy lives on because their love for freedom and justice was greater than their fear of death.

It is often said that we cannot love another until we love ourselves, but it is just as meaningful to say that we cannot love ourselves until we love another, whether that other is a person, a community or a visionary dream. Love extends us beyond the individual ego into dimensions that transcend mere survival.

The death of someone who loves life is not, therefore, the same as the death of someone who fears life. One will give themselves to their death in the same way they gave themselves to life; the other will contract away from death, perhaps trying to deny it is happening. Hermann Hesse wrote: 'The call of death is a call of love. Death can be sweet if we answer it in the affirmative, if we accept it as one of the great eternal forms of life and transformation.' Yet to discover this sweetness we need to love something over and above ourselves. This other may be a person, an animal, our family, justice, freedom, truth, a visionary possibility or even life itself, but it takes courage to love like this. We become willing to die for what we love.

It is a great and mysterious paradox that death renders life so precious, love renders us willing to die so that those we love can live.

To be committed to life does not mean we are terrified of death; it means that up until the point of our dying we are naturally afraid of it and struggle and fight for life, our life and the life of others, with the whole of our being. But when death is upon us, we accept death and surrender to it. Peter Brookes wrote in his autobiography that he had discovered the art of living lay in being utterly committed to the spot one was standing on and yet to be willing, in a moment, to let that go. This is the art of living because it is also the art of dying.

Yet in life and in death, fear interferes with both the commitment and the surrender. Though what is there truly to be afraid of in death? Anguish dies, fear dies, struggle dies, our separate ego dies, alienation dies, all physical pain dies, yet many aspects of who and what we have become while alive live on. And those parts may be our greater parts – our love, our creations, our consciousness, our wisdom, our humour, our legacy, what people have loved and remember of us.

It is another paradox; death is something to fear for the individual self, it is literally the end of all that matters, yet death is also a natural phenomenon and, when our time comes, nothing to be afraid of.

In one of the vivid dreams I am crawling through a tunnel dug out of dirt. Twigs and bits of branches are sticking through the earth and it could all collapse at any moment. I am muddy and dirty and crawling on my knees, which is difficult because I am holding up a baby Tim. My arms are tired and aching from the effort of holding him up so that he does not get mud and dirt over him. I am filthy, covered in mud, my hair matted, but at least Tim is relatively clean. I do not know if I will manage to hold him all the way through this tunnel as my arms feel like they are falling off. I crawl painfully slowly towards the light. My arms are screaming to put this baby down, yet although some soil and dirt has fallen on him, I am determined to shelter him from as much of the dirt as I can. At last we reach the opening of the tunnel and there is daylight. With one last superhuman effort, I hold Tim up to the opening and pass him up into the light. I sink back into the darkness of the tunnel utterly exhausted. But I have done my job.

To my surprise Tim transforms into a great light being with wings. He reaches down and pulls me up into the daylight. I am filthy, covered in mud, twigs in my hair, and completely shattered – but we are both out of the tunnel and in the light. We start to laugh. Dirt, tragedy, tears and twigs are suddenly the funniest things imaginable. We fall about helpless with laughter, gasping for breath. This whole drama has been utterly absurd. This muddy woman with messy grey hair and this angel of light with great wings are each as ludicrously preposterous as the other. We are both completely and gloriously ridiculous. We howl with laughter, with no thought for squashed wings, dirty clothes, rhyme or reason because our crawl through dark tunnels and into the light is suddenly one of the funniest things in the universe. And as for death, well death has become the most absurd joke of them all.

But when I woke I was not laughing. In the realms where Tim still lived, in my heart, in my dreams, in the silence of the moment, in shared memories with others, in the vast freedom of emptiness, I can laugh at death. In a world where in all directions Tim has gone, his body destroyed and his absence so potently present, death remained no laughing matter. Yet even though death is inconsolable loss, this is life. Death is life.

It is natural to fear death, but we do not need to be terrified of it, unless we are terrified of life. Fear is a useful instinct. It is a survival tool that helps us deal with physical threat. When adrenaline flows, our senses and reactions are more sensitive and alert. Yet in our modern technologically sophisticated world, our fears and anxieties tend to be more about what might happen rather than what is happening. The snapped twig that is a sign of a stalking tiger is no longer what frightens us; we are more afraid of not having enough money to pay our bills, becoming ill, losing our jobs, our hair or our position in society. But these events are usually possibilities in the future rather than actualities in the present and so the adrenalised body, which has evolved to deal with threats in the here and now, has a problem. Our brilliant capacity to construct possible futures, which has given us so much power to manipulate our environment, has also meant we now have to live with an anxiety that cannot be released through action.

We can certainly do what we can to avoid unpleasant futures and 'be prepared', but we cannot control everything. Therefore we have to learn to live with the anxiety that accompanies our capacity to construct potential futures in our minds.

One way we deal with our natural fear of death is to repress the uncomfortable feelings of anxiety and dread and substitute false hope. We imagine we are not afraid of death because we choose to believe that death is a return home where we live as a free spirit in a continuously wonderful feeling of love and light, or whatever version of the afterlife appeals to us most. But this is not death. This is a consoling belief in which it is imagined that the person believing it somehow continues. But that person dies. Aspects and energies may live on in various ways, but not the person, not the one that says 'I believe this', that one disintegrates. And this is the death that, naturally, we fear.

Another way we live with our existential anxiety is to project our anxiety on to an event even further in the future, ultimately our death. We project on to death a range of unresolved fears and anxieties that are more about issues and situations in life than about death. Some people say all fear is really a fear of death, but it is more true to say that all fear is really a fear of life.

Our most intimate fear is of ourselves. We are afraid of the sensations and feelings within ourselves that appeared too threatening when they first arrived, when we were young and with little power to change things. We then project on to death all the threatening possibilities in life that we could not deal with when we first experienced them, being overwhelmed, trapped, annihilated, rendered powerless, helpless, living in hopeless despair... Whatever scenario we have spent our lives trying to avoid, that is what we will project on to death. And the exact nature of our fears will be different for each of us.

If we look at what frightens us most about death, we often find a range of scenarios that reflect unresolved fears from our lives that are not about death at all. This usually involves what frightened us as children and led to the construction of our protective egos in the first place. And, as what we are ultimately afraid of is the feelings and sensations within ourselves, it is yet another paradox: we fear death because it is the end of our life energy, yet we fear death because we fear our life energy. We are afraid of losing what we have never allowed ourselves.

The root of our fear is the ego because it is the ego that controls life to avoid what we fear and it is this ego that is annihilated on death. But the individual ego-'I' that dies is not all of us. Our conscious awareness, our life energy, our freedom and our love extend beyond the individual self, and in the same way the body dies yet the greater Body of life does not, the ego dies but this extended-'I' does not. The extended-'I', therefore, has no fear of death.

During the civil wars in feudal Japan, an invading army would quickly sweep into a town and take control. In one particular village, everyone fled just before the army arrived – everyone except the Zen master. Curious about this old fellow, the general went to the temple to see for himself what kind of man this master was. When he wasn't treated with the deference and submissiveness to which he was accustomed, the general burst into anger.

'You fool,' he shouted as he reached for his sword, 'don't you realise you are standing before a man who could run you through without blinking an eye!'

'And do you realise,' the master replied, 'that you are standing before a man who can be run through without blinking an eye?'

Only someone who has confronted his or her fear can stare into the face of death without blinking. One of the best preparations for death, therefore, is to encounter each and every one of our fears consciously. This means noticing when we feel threatened and checking out whether our fear is real or imagined. It means we feel our fear and then either do it or not do it depending on the circumstances. It means noticing automatic reactions to situations and people and experimenting with behaving differently. It means engaging life in all its aspects, not only trying to control life to get what we want. It means learning the art of war *and* the art of surrender. It means freeing up our energy from being trapped in the past and bringing it into the present.

With less fear of death we become free to die with grace and dignity rather than in panic and terror. Our final act, when we give all that we have become and created back to life as we die, might even be an orgasmic joy – there is a reason the French call an orgasm 'le petit mort'. But before we can embrace death with an open heart, first we must face our fear. Better to do this while alive, however, than on our deathbed, as then we will be confronted by everything we have feared anyway, but without being prepared.

Basically engaging our fear entails learning from our own experience so that we begin to live in reality rather than in the projected fears of our own minds. In other words the best preparation for death is to live life.

9

Dancing With Demons

Be yourself – that much you owe to God.
Osho

We might personify our fears of death as the wrathful deities of the bardos or devils in purgatory, but those demons and deities are us. In contemporary language they are personifications of our fears and unresolved energies, aspects of ourselves that we did not become conscious of while alive. *The Tibetan Book of the Dead* says we have the chance to confront and overcome our fears after death even if we have not dealt with them while alive because in the seven weeks after death a Truth Body is formed. This is the manifestation of who we truly are rather than our ego's ideas or delusions about ourselves. This Truth Body then encounters the various demons and deities of the Death Realm, and how we relate with them determines our next reincarnation or whether we are liberated from the cycle of life and death completely.

In modern culture we might say that we are not judged by a Supreme Being or wrathful demons, we are answerable only to our own integrity. I am the only one who knows if I am lying or telling the truth, if my motives are genuine or manipulative, if I am afraid or not – others can only guess. I am therefore the only one who can judge me. But whatever language or images we use to describe this process of encountering the truth of oneself, death is the final reckoning. There is no escaping the reality of ourselves on death even if we have managed to avoid it through our life, because when we die our ego defences dissolve and we become who we truly are rather than the fictions and pretences we created while alive.

Those who work with the dying recognise the release of our true energy from the inhibitions of our controlling ego; its medical term is 'terminal restlessness'. The website for the charity Hospice Alliance describes it:

Patients may be too weak to walk or stand, but they insist on getting up from the bed to the chair, or from the chair back to the bed. Whatever position they are in, they complain they are not comfortable and demand to change positions, even if pain is well managed. They may yell out using uncharacteristic language, sometimes angrily accusing others around them. They appear extremely agitated and may not be objective about their own condition. They may be hallucinating, having psychotic episodes and be totally out of control. Some patients may demand to go to the hospital emergency room, even though there is nothing that can be done for them there. Some patients may insist that the police be called... that someone unseen is trying to harm them. Some patients may not recognise those around them, confusing them with other people. They may act as if they were living in the past, confronting an old enemy. Those who work with the dying know this type of restlessness or agitation almost immediately. However, the patient's family may have no idea what is going on and often become quite alarmed at their loved one's condition.

Modern care for the dying is often geared around a fear of death and, when their unresolved energies such as anger and terror start to manifest, people in this 'terminal restlessness' tend to be given tranquillizers and anti-psychotic medication. This is done from care, to calm the person down, ease his or her struggle, and to ease the anguish of their families, but it interferes with aspects of our dying.

Dying is a transition from self-control and self-regulation into a complete let-go. Although our ego's control is an essential aspect of human culture and necessary while living in society, on death we move into the ultimate freedom of never having to restrict or suppress our energy ever again. As we approach death, energies and impulses, which we may have kept locked up inside us all our lives, are allowed expression without restraint. This energetic freedom is a powerful and important let-go. It releases us from a lifetime's tension. It brings us more potently into the present. It brings denied energies back into life so that our death becomes a real death, not the half death that follows a half-life. It is a paradox: as we approach death, we come more alive as ourselves. But this means that whether we 'rage against the dying of the light' or smile in sweet surrender, we will have a living death, a whole death, *our* death.

This release of our energy is significant because, if we have not done it before, as our true energy becomes apparent, we can encounter our unresolved conflicts and our fears. This is important because just as we give what has been created by our love and consciousness back to life as we leave it, so we bequeath our unresolved energies, our resentments, envy, rage, insensitivity, cruelties, ignorance and greed. If we have not encountered and resolved these aspects of ourselves before we die, we can leave behind us disarray and confusion that someone else then has to resolve for us.

A friend died and his wife found emails to another woman in his computer that he had not deleted revealing that he had been having a secret affair. Another friend had to clean up the mess left behind by her aunt who had lived as a recluse surrounded by piles of disgusting rubbish. Another friend's father left an unfair will that divided the family in two. A woman told me that when her mother died she discovered the woman she thought was her mother was in fact her aunt and her biological mother had died many years previously; there was now no chance to find out more about her origins which compounded her grief.

Often our children carry the invisible legacies of our unresolved conflicts and feelings and we can be released only when they resolve these issues for us. Either that or they pass them on to *their* children to resolve. The family silver is passed down the generations above ground; underground more invisible legacies are bequeathed. These hidden unresolved aspects of our lives form a legacy just as much as our love and creativity.

The First Law of Thermodynamics, in this universe anyway, states: energy can neither be created nor destroyed, only transformed. In this context it implies that if we do not resolve our energy and feelings within ourselves, on death those energies do not just disappear; freed from the control of the ego as it dissolves, they begin to manifest. This can happen through the emotional outbursts, chaotic sounds and movements, irrational thoughts, unpredictable reactions to people and situations of the 'terminal restlessness'. We might say of that person 'they are not themselves'; the truth is they are becoming *more* themselves. Aspects they never expressed are being freed from the dying ego's control and lived out.

A close friend was given six weeks to live. He planned his death at home. He told me he was going to die as he had lived, as a samurai, and simply dissolve into stardust. But living as a samurai means you develop certain aspects but not others. As he lay dying, this man's unresolved energies and feelings came home to roost. Many of these could not be resolved by the stoicism of the samurai and overwhelmed him. He was given an anti-psychotic drug to calm him down. Within ten minutes of the drug being administered a man suffering from schizophrenia crashed his car into the side of my friend's house screaming – 'Kill me, kill me – I want to die!' The unresolved energies had been let loose and had to find another way to resolve themselves than within the consciousness of my friend.

Sometimes this acting out happens not through the behaviour of that person, particularly if drugs have been given to sedate them, but through another susceptible person, such as the schiz-ophrenic who crashed his car. Sometimes unresolved energies manifest through natural phenomena. One woman told me when her husband died a wind suddenly sprung up and blew ferociously around the house even though there was no wind anywhere nearby. Another man described how at exactly the time his wife died, a mirror fell off the wall and smashed into pieces. There are many tales of similar events when someone dies, because unresolved energies do not just fade away, they seek to be resolved in whatever way they can.

The resolution of unresolved energies in a dying person can happen through a journey with a shaman, a ceremonial rite or a religious ritual, with prayers, chanting, incantations and so on. But mostly in our modern world, this release happens through someone who has suffered directly from the dying person's unresolved anger, fear, greed or ignorance, someone who loves the dying person enough to suffer these for them – and forgives them. It is, after all, not a God in a far away heaven who really forgives us our sins; it is our fellow human beings, the ones we have hurt.

I know people who have sat by the side of a person they love as he or she dies, and have felt that person's unresolved anguish for him or her, because the dying person could not do this for his or her self. We might sit by a parent who has hurt us but never admitted it, yet still we stroke their hand. We might feel forgiveness for them even if they have never said sorry. In this way we are processing some of the dying person's unresolved issues for them. Sometimes we can do this before a person dies, sometimes it has to be afterwards. When my brother died I helped him after his death because it was not possible before.

Reincarnation is not the return of our individual self in another body, the same person with different coloured eyes speaking a different language, because this individual self is inextricably connected with this body, the one that dies and is gone forever. Re-incarnation for our multi-dimensional modern selves is the return to Earth of our unresolved conflicts and unfinished business, our hopes, fears, angers, passions and so on, in a multitude of ways that reflects our complexity. Not for us the simple successive reincarnations of more simpler psyches. Here is another reason to face up to our fears before we die; we become able to help those we love into their deaths, help them resolve aspects of themselves, as we are not afraid of the turbulence of death even if they are. Our love renders us willing to suffer their unresolved issues for them.

This process has been given many names – digesting our fears, eating our shadow, encountering our repressed energies, confronting our demons – yet however we describe the often painful process of facing up to the truth of ourselves, this is the spiritual journey that best prepares us for death. We extend beyond the ego-I and its fears into an expanded-I that is aware of our interconnected interdependence. We open to life beyond our personal concerns. We engage fully with whatever situation we encounter. We give ourselves to our family, our friends, music or art, a vision of justice, an appreciation of nature, whatever it is we are drawn to. And this is the expansion beyond the ego-I that cooks up our soul.

Soulful-ness is created in our struggles to live with integrity and dignity in ways that honour life in a world that ruthlessly pursues individual goals of power, status and money. We need our ego-I to survive, we live in a jungle as much as in a garden, yet the spirit of humanity lives beyond it. When we have loved beyond our own ego concerns, beyond our fear, beyond our personal desires, that love creates our soul and our legacy. Just as life is about more than survival, death too is about more than the end of our survival. Death is about love, consciousness, truth, freedom, so many things. Though for each one of us our death will be unique. What happens will depend on what we had the courage to love.

In one of the last vivid dreams I am walking alone along the ridge of a fell. The wind is warm and I feel strong and healthy as I clamber over the rocks. Below me sheep are calling to each other. Suddenly I can see Tim is ahead of me standing to the left of the path. He smiles as I run towards him.

'Tim, Tim, how wonderful to see you!'

We hug each other and, even though I am delighted to see him, the tears flow because I know he is dead. We link arms and walk together in an easy familiarity. There is nothing to say now because it has all been said. The path meanders between rocks, worn into smooth mounds by the wind, rain, dust and the unknown history of millennia. The windswept bushes rustle in the wind. Stonechats call. Bees murmur in the heather. Even on this high ridge there are butterflies. A robin sings on a blackthorn. I am walking with my dead son through a landscape full of life.

It occurs to me that Tim has died to the world, but not to life. He is alive in this dream. He is alive in me. He is alive in nature. He is alive because while he was alive he came to life utterly and completely. He loved. He struggled. He danced. He suffered. He created. He became his own unique self in so many aspects he cannot die. Not all of him anyway. Death is only annihilation for those who never lived. Come alive while you are alive and you will be alive in some form or other after you have died.

Tim laughs.

'You're getting it, Mum.'

We reach a point where the path forks. One path goes down to the left and the other heads up further along the ridge. Tim stops and disengages his arm.

'This is where we must go separate ways.'

I do not want this but I know it has to be.

Tim reaches out and holds my hands in his.

'It is only for a while. Then we will meet again. Differently.'

I nod but cannot speak. Tears are welling up inside me. If I had spoken I could not have restrained my weeping; I would have clung to him and, in the desperation of a mother's grief, would have refused to leave this death. But to choose death while alive is a betrayal of the deeper river within which Tim and I are finding each other again. Which means I must leave and walk into another loss in the long goodbye that is death.

I silently take the other path. Tim watches me as I walk back down into the valley but I do not look back. I would cry too many tears and turn into a pillar of salt. But I know he is standing there looking at me as I walk away. I know he is standing very still as I grow smaller and smaller into the distance. I know he is waiting until I have vanished from sight, and then he will continue his separate journey.

I woke from that dream, my pillow wet with tears and an old Scottish song in my head, one traditionally played at the end of an evening's revelry, dinner party or dance. Even in Scottish clubs, when the dance beats have stopped throbbing, this is the last song. 'Oh ye'll tak' the high road and I'll tak' the low road, and I'll be in Scotland afore ye, for me and my true love will never meet again on the bonnie bonnie banks of Loch Lomond.' It is the last song of a Jacobite Highlander, who is to be hung at dawn. The high road runs through the gleans, the beinns and the lochs, above ground; the low road is for the dead, the route home through the underworld. Five of Tim's great-grandparents were Scottish, most of the others were Irish, maybe our Celtic ancestors were singing to me.

Though in this dream I had taken the low road, Tim the high one. Perhaps because I was still subject to the gravitational pull downwards while Tim was free to rise above the heavy weight of matter. Perhaps because I had to go back down into the turbulence of life on Earth while Tim could float upwards into the peace that passes all understanding. But perhaps also because, unlike in the song, I have no doubt that Tim and I will meet again by another kind of loch when I die. Why this should be I cannot explain, but I do know that Tim lives on in me as I take him back into life, and I am with Tim as he takes me into his death. We are together in both worlds.

We remain connected with those we love even across the great divide of death. And though the dead and the living inhabit different worlds, we are together in that love. Our legacy becomes whatever we have had the courage to love. We could say, the dead do not leave their legacy behind them – they become it. Some aspects live on in the turbulence of our unresolved issues in the lives of those who knew us. Other aspects live on as a legacy of the spirit that is eternal. But, whatever the form, our legacy is created through love and is love. We become love.

Love is the gift of oneself. Such a giving transcends death because love leaves a legacy that makes one's life greater than one's death. That is the triumph of love over death – not that one survives, but that what one has created lives on. Love renders one's life greater than one's death.

10

I Sing the Body Electric

Most people think great god will come from the sky,
Take away everything and make everybody feel high.
But if you know what life is worth,
You will look for yours on earth.
The last song Bob Marley played on stage.

The body dies. We can all recognise death when we see it – the body has no movement or breath, no colour in its cheek or warmth in its touch, no light in its eyes or welcoming smile, only the cold still pallor of death. But as Bob Marley sang elsewhere in the above song, 'Half the story has never been told.' Just as the ego is not all of who we are, the body we think is our body, the flesh and blood body that dies, is not the whole story.

The body that lives in time eventually reaches the end of its time and dies, yet there is another Body that cannot die. This is the Body we had to leave in order to go on the great journey of becoming an individual human being. But on death we return to that Body, the source, the Body of all life. For the other animals this presents no problem. They do not go through the socialization process of developing an individual ego as have we humans, as a consequence they unconsciously know that death is just the transformation of life into life. We do not. We are more aware that death is the end of our individual life.

Yet we are also animals. Even if we are not consciously aware of it, our body has not forgotten its interconnectedness with all life. Our body 'knows' that when we breathe and eat this is the continual interpenetration of life with life, and that although a life can end, life itself does not. This is why learning to connect with the hidden wisdom of the body is one of the best preparations for death. But what do we mean by 'the wisdom of the body'? One thing for sure is that it will not be a knowledge or wisdom that can be spoken; the body communicates through energy not words, feeling not thought.

We think of the body as an object, but the body is not a thing; it is a constant flow of energy. The body is life. Life is a constant flow. Out of this river of life, our human mind creates a world of separate objects, each with its own existence in time and space. This division of the energy flow of life into separate objects allows us to name and manipulate things, to create technologies and machines, to identify ourselves as unique individuals; it also entails a separation from the interdependency and communion of life where there is no death, only continually changing form. This is the one-ness we came from and into which we return on death. Death is the end of all alienation and existential aloneness and as much as we are afraid of it, there are parts of us that long for it.

I spent many years as a disciple of Osho Rajneesh. I gave myself utterly and completely to this journey. I was seeking many things, a life based on love rather than money, on freedom rather than power, a way of living in harmony with others, the environment and all the creatures of this Earth; I was also hoping to end up enlightened, a state that I imagined as a lifelong happiness with no more pain, fear or torment, my own psycho-spiritual version of the American Dream – except that thousands of us were dreaming it.

For a while we really were living the dream. We were not only the chosen few, spiritually evolved and almost enlightened, we were sexy, knew the latest dance moves and partied hard. It didn't appear to get better than this. But like all dreaming not grounded in the actual reality of life on a planet with north and south poles, hot and cold, in and out, light and dark, life and death, aspects of our dream turned into a nightmare. I ended up encountering all that I had been hoping to escape right in the heart of my very attempts to escape it – of course. And thank goodness. Though I must admit, I didn't appreciate it at the time.

Chogyam Trungpa, the Tibetan Rinpoche who first brought Tantric Buddhist teachings to the West, said, 'Enlightenment is like a cow-pat falling on your head.' He made it clear that enlightenment is not a land of milk and honey, a return to the Garden of Eden or the happy ever after I had fondly imagined. It is not even something to strive for. It is something that happens to us – like death. In a way, enlightenment *is* death. It is a return to the oneness beyond all duality that is the end of us as separate self-determining individuals. 'Not my will but thine be done.' This is the death of the ego.

We project our hopes onto whatever is our version of the 'good' life: happy families, success, fame, wealth, enlightenment... And we project our fears on to death: being heartbroken, sad, overwhelmed, annihilated, helpless... But neither the 'good' life nor death is likely to turn out to be what we have hoped or feared. A real enlightenment involves the realisation that this is it – it is all happening here not there, now not then. Enlightenment and death have a lot in common. A death too involves the truth of ourselves unfolding and revealing itself here and now.

All meditation, in the end, brings us face to face with death. For example the Zen koan 'What is your original face before your parents were born?' takes us beyond our identity as a separate body and into a realisation that we are part of the greater Body of all life. Which is what happens on death anyway whether we are aware of this or not. The journey of meditation reveals that really we never left; we just think we did. If you look into the eyes of a newborn baby, you will see your original face, the face of the Body that cannot die, the Body we came from and into which we will return on death.

A baby makes no differentiation between itself and anything else. It has no idea of itself as in any way separate from the totality of life within it and all around it. William James called this a 'booming, buzzing confusion', Freud, 'polymorphous perversity', and Rousseau, 'tabula rasa'. However we name it, for a baby everything is one body. But gradually the young child is socialised into human culture and learns that the human world is composed of a multitude of objects separated in time and space – including his or her self.

Every child has to leave the Garden of Eden all over again to enter human culture. They have to leave behind the undifferentiated flow of life, dividing it into good and evil, and live in a world of objects separated in time and space, including themselves. They construct the idea of an object that is 'me', an ego, and an object out of the flow of energy that is the life of the body, an objectified body that is 'mine'. But this body lives in time and therefore dies. When a child learns about his or her own separate existence, they discover self-awareness and freedom, but also loneliness and death.

Eventually we forget there is another way of being and our division of energy into things, union into separate-ness and the endless moment into chronological time become what we believe are the only realities. We find new freedoms but also find we are profoundly alone. We are divided from each other. We are divided within ourselves. And we are exiled from the simple bliss of one-ness where there was no death, into the awful knowledge that we will die. As Malcom X said, 'The price of freedom is death.'

Each child has to make the journey from one-ness to aloneness, from belonging to all life to belonging to oneself, all over again. Weaning involves losing far more than the breast. D W Winnicott, the famous child psychoanalyst, said that a child is ready to begin weaning when they initiate games that involve throwing toys out of the pram or high-chair. The toys roll away and disappear, until the mother finds them again and gives them back. The loss of an object and its return is the playing that prepares them for the loss of the breast, the symbol of the greater Body of which one is part.

Tim loved this game. He'd throw back his head and laugh until he was almost hysterical as cups, plates, cutlery, toys, clothes, scraps of paper were lost and then found. He loved this lost-and-found game so much, he continued it long after he had let go of even his last bedtime breast-feed. He hid things under cushions, behind chairs, on top of shelves and ordered me to find them. I'd have to hide things while he looked. Then he'd hide himself for me to find and I'd have to hide from him. The game evolved. He'd hide and not tell me he was hiding – how long would it take me to notice he'd gone? Would I drop everything and begin looking for him? How long would I search before I gave up? Loss and rediscovery. Absence and presence. Nothing and something. We played the lost-and-found game over and over, at home and later across the world. Later still we played it in its ultimate form – across the great divide of death. Eventually I found him again, not in the separate body that dies, in another Body, the one our animal bodies never left, the Body of all life. Where, as I discovered, we all meet.

After scattering Tim's ashes, on his birthday, nearly a year after he had died, his friends organised a party. Friends who could not come to his funeral had time to organise themselves for this. They travelled from all over the world to be there.

His friends arrive, from school, from university, people who had met him on the road and never forgotten him, who had had adventures with him into the night in cities spread across the globe, people who had worked with him, partied with him, flown off to far flung places all over the world with him – people who had loved him, people who he had loved. Every floor is packed and the party is spilling out on to the streets. The music is thumping out its beat, the drink is flowing, the food is plentiful. This is more like a birthday party than a wake. Which, after all, is exactly what it is, Tim's last birthday party.

Someone shouts out over the music – look there's Tim! We turn and stare. Above the door is a stuffed fox's head, wearing a flat cap at the same angle Tim used to, with sunglasses like the ones Tim wore. This foxy-tim looks down on us, presiding over his party, with a wicked grin exactly like Tim's. Of course! Tim would never miss his own party.

This is a young person's scene and soon it is time for Martin and me to leave. We stand and pull on our jackets. I look around the room jammed with young people laughing, dancing, joking, playing; they are so alive the goodness of it is a sweet high. Tim is here. Tim's spirit is living in the dance and play of his friends. I can see Tim in their gestures, their dance moves, the swoops and dives of their laughter, their hugs and gesticulations, their shining eyes when they speak of Tim, of how grateful they are to have known him, how much they had loved him, how they will never forget him. And they won't. This body of young people, so bright and beautiful, is the greatest testament possible to Tim's life.

Martin and I weave towards the front door through more hugs and laughter. Chris' fiancée arrives just as we leave. He introduces us. I hug and congratulate them with not a shadow in my celebration of their love and future. How can there be? Their happiness is Tim's.

Martin and I slip out the door leaving this partying Sangha to its festivities. Tim is dead. Long live Tim.

The other animals never left the simplicity of this Eden, where all is one body of life in this moment, but we cannot live as the other animals do. To live in our complex human communities we have had to create laws rather than merely trusting our instincts. We internalise the rules of right and wrong by controlling the natural flow of energy through our body through tension in our muscles, restricted breathing and control over spontaneous movement. This bodily tension is the physical counterpart of the psychological ego.

On death the tension of the ego's will and self-control dissolve, which is why death looks like an annihilation to the parts of us that live in tension. Yet just as when we die, the ego dies, but the ego is not all of us, the tension of these controls over our energy dies, but this is not all of us. Our energy does not die. It is transformed. Death is the ultimate surrender of our will to the reality of the energy of the body.

Death is not annihilation; it is the transformation of one form of life into another. The body we think is the body we are is the collection of fearful tension that is our ego – and this body dies. The animal body we truly are is a body of subtle sensitivity and feeling, the body electric, a flow of energy – and this Body cannot die, it can only be transformed. But we have become identified with our patterns of control over our energy, our ego. And in this is the difficulty, because on death there is no more tension or control of any kind. On death the body surrenders completely to the processes of life, which, of course, includes death.

Other animals do not have internal conflict as they approach death because they do not impose their individual will on to the natural energy of their instincts. An animal can be trained to behave how we want them to but not because they internalise rules of right and wrong. They have no knowledge of good and evil and simply revert to their natural instincts if we are not there to control them. We, on the other hand, have to fragment the natural integrity of the animal we are in order to become human and develop a morality with an understanding of right and wrong. We have to turn away and betray the animal body even though it is the animal body that gives us life. It was, after all, the instincts of sexuality in the animal bodies of our parents that brought us to life in the first place. But once we have turned away and abandoned the animal body, from then on we live in fear of death.

The animal body itself does not fear death. Animals experience death of course, but they do not know they will die while they are alive. An animal will fight to the death for life, but not because it is afraid to die, because it is utterly committed to life. When we humans die, however, it is more complex. We know that death ends our individual life. And to the degree we are identified with our separate existence rather than our inter-connectedness with others, this creates worries and anxieties in us that other animals do not have.

> *Two cows are in a field. First Cow: 'Do you worry about getting Mad Cow Disease?' Second Cow: 'Nah, I'm a penguin.' 'No worries then.' 'Except for why I'm hanging out with a gorilla.' 'Are you blind? I'm a bat.' 'Ah, no worries then.'*

Animals may experience anxiety, especially if they are around anxious human beings, but it is a temporary anxiety connected with environmental conditions, not the chronic existential anxiety we humans know. But we too are animals. In fact we can be human only to the degree we can be animal. Even though as humans we have identified ourselves with being a particular object rather than the flow of life, the instincts of our animal bodies hold the living knowledge that death is simply the endless transformation of life into life. But this knowledge is usually unconscious.

The unconscious is not an abstract idea; it is an embodied reality, the energy of the living, feeling flow of life outside our ego's constraints. The body is the unconscious. The body is our instinctual aliveness and life energy beyond the inhibitions and tensions of our conditioning, beyond our identification with a specific body, beyond all our self-control and will. This uncon-scious body is what keeps us alive. The continuous working of our liver and kidneys, the tidal ebb and flow of our hormones, every breath that transmutes O_2 into CO_2, the neural networks of our central nervous system, the billions of microorganisms in our gut, these form us, *are* us, beyond our conscious mind. This is the living, breathing, pulsing animal body with aeons of evolution behind it. And this living energy is connected with the greater Body of all life that survives our individual death. Our animal body knows how to die even if the human parts of us do not.

The animal body is one of our greatest teachers in the art of dying because the surrender to death is the same as the surrender to the life flowing through our animal bodies while alive. The art of dying is the same as the art of dancing, making love, breathing, enjoying a sunset, laughing with friends, playing with animals, singing, crying, howling or sitting in silence with full awareness of the life all around us, all of which involve a surrender to the natural instincts of the body. The animal body will teach us everything we need to know about how to die – though first we must surrender to it. Then we become able to die in the knowledge that death is the sacred and mysterious renewal of life into more life. Which is a different death from one in terror of annihilation.

The ego, the body of tension and control that has enabled us to live in the human world, has alienated us from our natural life force and therefore our natural death process. Yet this very alienation from our natural selves has enabled us to look back at ourselves and know that we are alive, rather than simply being alive as are the other animals, and therefore also to know that we will die. It is a paradox: the creation of human self-consciousness alienates us from our lives and deaths, yet this is also what gives life and death meaning and significance.

On death, our separation from the whole is ended, duality is dissolved and we return to the one Body of all life anyway, whether or not we have consciously realised this before we die. But if we can re-embrace the energies of our body and see our 'original face' before we die, then we can surrender to death without fear.

One of the most potent methods to prepare for a death without terror and panic is to consciously re-embrace the animal body while we are alive. And if we connect with the instincts and energies of the body while we are alive, the process of dying can be a conscious engagement rather than the unconscious disintegration that terrifies us. Then we can surrender to the processes of death in the knowledge that our death is part of life's evolution rather than solely the ending of our life. And we die, not in a struggle with death, in a surrender into life.

Tim had been dead a month. I had thought about nothing but his death. I was struggling. How could it be right that I was alive while my son was dead? I knew that Tim would not want me to spend the rest of my life in mourning but how could I enjoy life when he was dead? How could I have any pleasure in life, enjoy the sun and the sounds of birdsong, laugh with friends over dinner and a bottle of wine, when Tim can have none of these ever again? I lay back in the sun and closed my eyes.

I feel a tap on my shoulder.

When we walked together, Tim would frequently reach around my shoulders with his long arm and tap my far shoulder. I would turn and he would laugh and I would pinch him to get my own back. We had done this for as long as I can remember. At least as long as his arms were long enough. This time I hear Tim say: 'Come with me!'

He throws three stars into the sky and leaps on to one for a ride. I leap on to another and we ride our stars on a roller coaster ride through the cosmos. We sweep in huge cosmic circles surrendering to the movement of the stars in an ecstatic let-go. It is wonderful. We laugh and shout out with joy. Suddenly my mind comes in – what is going on? I become afraid and stop. Tim reins in his star. 'Don't worry, Mum, you'll learn.' He waves his arm. A thousand fireworks of light explode simultaneously and a fantastic kaleidoscope of colour fills the sky. It is utterly beautiful. Tim laughs as his fingers create moving lights and patterns that fill every part of the universe in a vast Aurora Borealis. I am staring transfixed when Tim breaks into song: 'Catch a falling star and put it in your pocket never let it fade away, 'cos love may come and tap you on the shoulder one starry night…' A cool hip-hop and reggae *man, Tim would **never** sing a song by Perry Como. 'You would not be seen dead singing that song!' I tell him. He laughs.*

I opened my eyes. Tim was playing among the stars.

Perhaps just as I could enjoy cosmic light shows and rides on stars through him, he could share some of the joys of life through me. I was beginning to realise, I had to find Tim in life and he had to find me in death. Just as I had to find Tim in death, and he had to find me in life.

That evening I went into the kitchen, poured myself a glass of Chablis and cooked dinner. I had been vaguely throwing together ingredients or sticking ready-made meals in the microwave; now I began to cook again. Between basting potatoes, shelling peas, whisking eggs and tasting the sauce, I sat in the evening sun on the bench outside our back door. And Tim was with me. He came every evening for about a month as I drank wine and cooked. We didn't say much. We had anyway pretty much said everything we ever needed to while he was alive. We sat together as the sun went down, making random toasts to life, nature, death, the stars, a mother and son who had lost each other, and then found each other again, many times over.

11

A Divine Mortality

Remember this: in the way you love is the way God will be with you.
Jalāl ad-Dīn Muhammad Rūmī

Love and consciousness are the most intimate and self-evident realities while also being two of the most transcendent and mysterious. And both love and consciousness are essential aspects of the mystery that is death.

A myth found in widely different cultures is of the central role human consciousness and love play in the unfolding destiny of the cosmos. For example the Australian Aborigines say humans must sing with open hearts to the sun each morning, else the sun will not rise. Siberian shamans say that humans provide nature with her order and, without us, even the plants would not know when to flower. This is because there is a sacred reciprocity between plants, who are here to serve us, and humans, who give nature its meaning with our love and awareness. And at the heart of the profound Christian myth is that the greatest God of them all had to become human in order to create the love the world needs to redeem itself. Because it is not the gods who make the love and consciousness the cosmos needs, we do.

Gods already have everything they need; we, on the other hand, do not. We are the ones who suffer our humanity and in doing so create the love that saves us from ourselves. Organised religions keep God in his heaven until we are ready to take on that responsibility, and that freedom, for ourselves. Various esoteric sects have known this throughout history. The secret rites of the Eleusinian Mysteries took you through a ritual death into the revelation that we are the very gods we once worshipped. The secret knowledge of the Sufis, for which you would be killed if you revealed it, is: 'I am God.' Even Jesus said: 'I am the way, the truth and the life' and, as Barry Long so often pointed out, there is only one 'I' in the whole universe – the one each of us says for ourselves. And so if we do not create love and consciousness, no one else will. Though it is easier to give this task to the gods than take responsibility for it ourselves.

The difference between gods and humans is that gods are immortal and humans are mortal. We die; our gods do not. The perennial mistake we humans make, with our awful knowledge of death, is to assume that to discover the secret of eternal life we have to become like a god or an angelic being full of light. The truth is that to encounter that which does not die, we have to become even more fully human – and die.

Neither love nor consciousness has meaning without death; death is therefore central to the order and right workings of the cosmos. As we have seen, only a creature divided from itself can look back at itself and become aware that it is alive rather than just being alive, and simultaneously, therefore, aware of the possibility of *not* being alive, of being dead. And only such a self-conscious creature, aware of itself and life, becomes able to live life in love and consciousness, and therefore also its opposite, fear and ignorance. Love and death are inextricably entangled with the very consciousness that makes us human.

There is a story of Lucifer different from the one I was taught by the nuns at my convent school. When God finished making Adam and Eve, he ordered Lucifer, the brightest of all the angels, whose name means 'bringer of light', to bow down before these frail and mortal human beings. Lucifer refused, saying he would bow down only to God. For this he was expelled from Heaven and entered the Hell he rules as Satan. In this story it was not his pride or competitiveness with God that led to his exile from paradise; it was his ignorance of the power of vulnerability and mortality.

We, also, can imagine that the way to triumph over death is to become like a god, immortal and invulnerable. But that way we lose our only hope for eternity. Because the very qualities of being that transcend the finality of death are exactly those born out of our frail and imperfect humanity.

Twenty years before Tim died, I stayed for six months in a beautiful 17th century villa on the shores of Lago Maggiore complete with balconies, views to the Alps, towers, stone steps, terraces and courtyards, sweeping stairs and wide halls that led into elegant rooms with marble floors, antique chandeliers and painted ceilings. In this fading Renaissance splendour, sixty of us planned to explore the far reaches of human consciousness. We intended to enter the realms Zen monks reach through their Zazen and koans, indigenous peoples through hallucinogenic plants, shamans through trance dances, Hindus by yogic postures and chanting, Taoists through meditation and martial arts, and Judaeo-Christian-Islamic mystics through fasting and prayer. We were going to sample and re-mix bits of all of these, plus our own take on it all, which would include dancing and Tantric sex, to give birth to old understandings in a new form. That was the plan anyway.

What happened was amazing. Under the gaze of painted cherubs and the light reflected from ancient chandeliers in vast golden mirrors, other dimensions of being revealed themselves. We encountered forces of the universe beyond anything our intellectual minds could comprehend – or even begin to describe. But, we were running from our humanity, not embracing it. Like Lucifer when he refused to bow to the shivering mortals Adam and Eve, we did not understand the power of vulnerability.

Gods and angels, with their might and glory, are immortal. They are not vulnerable, cannot be mortally wounded, do not die. Their power and glory can shock and awe and make many things happen, their brilliant light can illuminate galaxies, but they cannot make love. Only we terribly frail mortals can do that, with our imperfections, insecurities, needs and inadequacies, our awful mistakes, the darkness in our hearts and our existential anxieties about death. We would not need love otherwise. You don't need love when you're immortal. You don't need anything. Though some adoration and worship might not come amiss.

Lucifer had looked down from his great height at these naked human creatures, shivering in awe of the magnificent light that clothed him in glory and had not understood he should bow before this terrible vulnerability. And neither, so often, do we. Yet even the almighty God of the Jews had to become human, able to be wounded and killed, in order to create the love that would redeem the suffering of this world.

The landscape of myth is the landscape of the human spirit and we are, each of us, Lucifer and Adam, Satan and Eve. If we want only half the story, then we must either murder our humanity to become divine, or kill our gods to render them human. We wanted to become like gods and so we began to kill our humanity. In trying to be like the immortal gods, without knowing what we were doing, a collective insanity unfolded.

As soon as I realised what was happening, I left. I locked the great gates to the spirit world and turned my back on those realms. I would say that incarnation matters more than transcendence, 'this very body the Buddha, this very Earth, the lotus paradise', here is where we take on the commitment to love one another, not there. And I was never going to venture into those other dimensions of reality again.

I returned to north London, created a home and turned at last to face my humanity and my family. Tim, Martin, and I met every Thursday evening for two years to deal with the fallout from my adventures to the far reaches of human consciousness. The understandings I had reached on the journey that had taken me so far away from them now became the vehicle through which we found each other again. All we had to do was share ourselves and let the love between us do the work.

We discovered that the love that heals us and redeems our mistakes does not lie far away in some other realm, the gift of a deity in his or her heaven or in an enlightened absence of human struggle; it is found in the daily reality of our relationships with each other in the midst of our frailties and imperfections. We discovered that family love, with all its confusions and mistakes, its failings and limitations, has the power to heal wounds that go back generations, to create even more love, and to cook up a consciousness that understands the importance of our common humanity because this is its source. Love may not be all we need, but we all need the human love that knows the suffering we can cause each other yet can also forgive.

However determined I was to turn my back on the Spirit World, however, and root myself solely in my humanity, Tim's death blew open the portals to other worlds all over again. And not only for me. About nine months after Tim's death, Martin had a dream.

'I was standing in front of two massive wrought iron gates. They were full of fantastic designs of mythical creatures, angels and demons. I knew this was the gate to the Spirit World. But they were closed and although I could see through them, I didn't know how to open them. Suddenly Tim appeared on the other side of the gates and flung them open. He stood there smiling, with arms wide open, very happy to see me, and I him. "Hello, Martin," he said. We hugged. He told me to come with him and we went through the gates. I was anxious but Tim was joking and playing around which helped me relax.

'He took me on a tour through fabulous landscapes and strange regions of existence where the forces of the universe do their thing. Disembodied beings, energies, nameless force fields of creation and destruction, we saw them all. It felt completely familiar to me. I realised I had often visited here when I was younger. In fact I was so at home in other realms of being, I began to use them as an escape from the *demands of physical reality. Which is why I had to turn my back on all that and enter the real world. But I have been so busy building up a business and making sure we have enough money, I've got a bit out of balance. In the dream Tim reminded me of so many things I've forgotten. It was a wonderful dream.*

'We walked back to the gates and hugged. I asked him: "Will you be coming to see me again?" He said: "No. It has been an effort for me to return to a physical shape to be with you but I did it to help you. So that you would know, whenever you need me I am here for you."

'I was very sad because I knew he was going further away into the formless. But I knew it was right.'

When Tim's death opened those great gates again, this time both Martin and I knew that love is central to this mystery – because we had seen what happens when it is not. Where love is not, that is hell. Without love, death has no resurrection, just the oblivion of endless night. As Auden wrote, 'we must love one another or die'. And this death is not only the death of the body; it is the death of our soul.

Ram Dass has often said: 'Never throw anyone out of your heart, and then be free to do whatever you wish.' When you love a person, an animal, a group, whatever, you have a great freedom with them. You can throw propriety to the winds and be ruthlessly honest. You can let go and be spontaneous without concern for the consequences. You can be yourself. You can even do your worst, and if it is done in the context of a love between you then, however profound the hurt, there will always be the understanding and forgiveness that is its redemption. And this love extends even across the divide of death.

Not long after Martin's dream of the Spirit World he had another. He told me:

'You and I are in a group of people at some kind of conference. Tim arrives. He has a gun. A massive gun. Even bigger than a Kalashnikov AK47. You go over to him and I am very worried because Tim could

shoot and kill you. Everyone stops what they are doing and stares at you and Tim with fear and dread. Tim raises the gun and begins to shoot. He shoots all around you, in a body-shape around your body, laughing and playing. He then hands the gun to you and you turn it on him and do exactly the same, shooting all around the shape of his body. You two are playing, laughing and having fun, but everyone else is totally terrified. Me too. Because of the power of the weapon and the fear that you will kill each other. But you two are simply falling about laughing, enjoying the play of it all. You know you will not hurt each other. You are having great fun and are thoroughly relishing the whole drama.'

I wept when Martin told me this dream. I wept because I knew that Tim and I had lived out our darkness on each other more than on anyone or anything else. We each had done our worst to the other. Yet there had been enough love to hold us until we came out the other side. And we emerged, as a result, with a love that gave each other absolute freedom to be. Thank God. Because such a love is forever. And this is the vajra love, the diamond love that is indestructible and which carried Tim and me into his death and through to the other side of it.

Tim had been dead five months and our first Christmas without him arrived. Tim loved Christmas and I was dreading the pain and anguish of his not being here. On Christmas Eve one of my sisters called. She told me that snow was covering their village of Melbourne. 'All our lives, we have wanted a white Christmas, it has never happened. I know it sounds crazy, Anne, but we are convinced it is Tim's Christmas present to us.' Before falling asleep that night I told Tim, I want a present too. In the night I had another vivid dream.

I meet Tim. We are in armchairs in a comfortable hotel. I sip a gin and tonic and he leans back with a brandy.

'Right, Mum, there's a few things I need to tell you,' he begins.

'I hope you're not going to give me a lecture,' I say.

He laughs. 'Just drink your G&T and listen.' He lights a cigarette. 'You and I, dear Mother, completed our mother-son journey with all the shifting balances of powers and vulnerabilities, right through to the very end. And what's more we did it magnificently.' He smiles at me. 'Really, Mum, you are being rather pathetic. You should be celebrating our relationship not berating yourself for your failings.'

I put my glass down. 'But you're only saying that because you're dead. I'm still alive. I am the one that abandoned you on my search for whatever and taught you to abandon yourself.'

He laughs. I can see nothing to laugh about.

'But, Mum, that is not what my death was about. Listen to me.' He leans forward. 'I would rather have had you as a mother than anyone else.' He grins. 'Just as you would rather have had me as a son than even a son who had children and lived until he was ninety – go on admit it!'

This time when he grinned at me, I smiled back. But I was not yet ready to give it to him, that his death was OK. Because it wasn't.

That same night I had another vivid dream.

Tim is three years old. I am in love with him, just as he is in love with me. I give him a bath, dress him, we play games and sing nursery rhymes, all the while we are loving each other. He reaches up, puts his little arms around my neck, snuggles in and kisses me. 'I love you, Mummy,' he says. 'And I love you too, Timmy,' I say. And we laugh and cuddle in the warmth and play of so much love.

Even in the dream I knew this to be true, that we deeply loved each other and always will. The heartbreak lay in that so many things came in between us. My searching. My ideologies. My hopes and fears. My desperate attempts to create a better world rather than learning to live in this one. The world came in between us. But I am learning our love has managed to digest everything that came between us. It has managed to digest the world. Now, there is nothing but the love that bridges even the great divide of death. And nothing can take this love away from us – not even death.

Love is the bridge between worlds, because when a person dies, our love for them does not. And neither, mysteriously, does theirs for us. Love is a real living energy, an embodied experience, a feeling, not only an abstract idea; and is at the heart of our human mystery. Love involves the anarchic instincts of our animal bodies and our highest spiritual longing for transcendence. It is at the root of our human predicament yet is also its creative resolution. While being intimate and private, love has tremendous cultural, social and transcendental dimensions. Love is a living energy and we create it.

We not only make the love that makes us, literally through making sexual love, we are continually creating the energy of love in a multitude of ways. Each time we give ourselves to someone or something beyond our individual ego, each time we encounter life or another in a vulnerable being-ness without defences, each time we are willing to suffer for another or something beyond ourselves, we contribute to a continually evolving energy-field of love. We create the death-less, the transcendental qualities of love and consciousness that form our soul.

Death is the dissolution of all separateness and a sacred coming together where we become members of each other. Death reveals that we belong to each other as much as to ourselves. And death shows us that this great body of belonging is love. Through death, we participate in the greatest mystery of all, that of love and the endless recreation of love in life. What comes into being through the God of Death is a God of Love. And it is we who become this God. We make the love that creates what is eternal. We become what will redeem us, forgive us our mistakes and give us eternal life. Whenever we love a person, a vision, a hope, a community, a principle, a quality, whatever it might be, enough to die for it, then we are creating what is death-less. Death therefore makes what we do while alive here on Earth as momentous as creation itself. Because without death there would be no love and no need for love and we would not be driven to create anything.

Yet though love comes into being through our vulnerable mortality and death, death cannot destroy love. And what death cannot destroy is what is eternal. Love is eternal life. It is one of the greatest of all paradoxes that death makes life so precious, our love makes us willing to die so others may live. Which is why, however powerful is death, in the end, love is even more powerful.

12

Conversations With the Goddess

And I will show that nothing can happen more beautiful than death.
Walt Whitman

Tim had been dead for two years yet I continued to feel a deep remorse that Tim's death was somehow my fault. I had seen the barren and loveless lives that surrounded me as a child (my childhood held a lot of insanity and pain) and had gone on a search for freedom, love, truth, enlightenment, liberation... the name changed but not the search. As a result I had not been the mother Tim had often needed, a mother who was reliable, steady, always there for him. Eventually I stopped running from my demons, and Tim and I had healed much of what had happened between us. Then he died and I felt I must have done too little, too late. My regret and remorse, that he had drunk and taken drugs with such abandon because of my mistakes as a mother, was killing me. I wanted to die.

A friend called. She asked how I was. 'I will never feel joy or happiness in being alive ever again,' I told her. 'You need to do an Ayahuasca ceremony with a shaman,' she told me. 'I will take you; it will be my gift to you.' Several weeks later we were in an Ayahuasca ceremony with a shaman.

Ayahuasca is a plant of the Amazonian rainforest. It is said by many shamans to be the most potent soul-medicine on the planet. Though used primarily as a religious sacrament, it is also used to heal physical ailments and emotional anguish of all kinds. We can name the realm of human experience beyond our intellectual minds the Spirit World, the collective unconscious, the numinous, the archetypal realm, the noosphere or simply the transcendental, but whatever we name it, throughout history, humanity has needed a connection with this realm to sustain and nourish our spirits. The bridge that connects these worlds in many cultures has been shamanic ritual using psychotropic plants.

For Ayahuasca a tea is brewed from a combination of two different plants, the wood of the vine of Banisteriopsis that contains MOAI, and a number of different plants that contain DMT, the most common being the leaves of Psychotria viridis (Chacruna). The spirit of this vine, the spirit of Ayahuasca, is said to be the gatekeeper and guide to other realms. The name Ayahuasca means 'Vine of Death'.

I did four Ayahuasca ceremonies over one year, each one a sacred experience beyond anything I could have imagined. It is almost impossible to communicate what happened as the experience unfolded within me on a profound energetic level beyond analysis and words; much of what I write is therefore metaphor not fact. I can only describe it, inadequately, by saying that I met an intelligence and wisdom that was not human, and many profound and healing processes unfolded within our encounter.

The shaman gives me the Ayahuasca tea. My intention is to be healed of the dreadful regret that my life with Tim led to his premature death from drink and drugs. I lie down in the dark and wait. But before any cure, a disease must first come to light.

Suddenly I see Tim as a very young child lying in his bed – he is calling out: 'Where is my mum?' I see him as a child of five, six, seven, and through into his teenage years as he lies in beds all over the world calling out to life – 'where is my mum?' I see that his book My Life in Orange *was in part this question. But I never heard him and so I never answered it. I never even heard it in his book. No one hears it. He is alone with both his loss and his searching.*

I am utterly heartbroken to see this. I weep. My pillow is wet with my tears. Of course I always made sure he was safe and with good people, but he wanted me not others, however kind. He wanted me to put him first, not love, enlightenment, global liberation or whatever else I thought mattered more than him, more than my family, more than myself. I have often told people I was the best of mothers and the worst of mothers; they hasten to reassure me. But I know what they do not. I loved Tim completely and gave him profound spiritual sustenance and freedom, yet I also left him time and time again as I went on the search for myself, life, God, love, freedom, whatever I called whatever it was I was seeking. Tim therefore had many nights, throughout his childhood, when he lay in bed without me there.

I weep in an agony of remorse and regret.

The Ayahuasca spirit comes to me dressed in writhing snakes. They surround me and curl around my legs and body; yet I am not afraid because I know I am in the presence of a potent and sacred medicine and that these snakes are her healing powers. 'Help me please,' I ask her. She tells me, 'Tim had a dead mother; that is why he could not find her. You had been killed. Tim could not find you in life, but he found you in death. You have now found each other completely and are together forever.' I ask her to explain. She told me, 'Tim had a dead mother. Though neither of you knew you were dead.' I do not understand. 'What do you mean I was dead?' 'You were killed before you even began. You were alive as a body and as energy, but not as a person.' She smiles. 'Though to be a dead person is not necessarily the terrible thing you imagine.' I am utterly bewildered by this but she is showing me the energetic truth of it and I cannot deny it. 'What happened? Who killed me? Why?' She tells me, 'Go and find out.' She points to the side and there is my mother. I ask her, 'Did you kill me?' 'No, though I saw it happen. But I was so caught up in my own dramas I did nothing to save you.' 'So who or what killed me?' She nods to her left and then I see the devastation that came into me through my father.

I do not see the actual events of my childhood, I see the inner destruction that was wreaked on my young self. I see that in my profoundly disturbed and unhappy family, as the eldest child, I took on caring for everyone. I see that in caring for everyone in the middle of so much insanity I lost connection with myself. Yet the depth of the dysfunction was utterly denied. We believed the insanity of the family was normal. I see myself being formed by the events of my childhood and watch this desperate young girl focus entirely on the compelling needs of her family and lose herself as a person. Her needs became irrelevant and the needs of the situation became all. I am seeing these things with a clarity that surpasses any insight or understanding I have reached before.

I see how my life became a quest, not for any specific goal or achievement, for something indefinable and intangible, something that I did not understand or even know about myself. I had been brought up in an insanity of unreality, what I was seeking was simply reality.

The Ayahuasca Spirit shows me more.

I see how the insanity in my family of origin affected my brother and sisters. I see its evil source in our family history. I see that we were all victims of something terrible and neither of my parents had the strength to do other than pass it on to their children to deal with. I see how Tim had had the worst kind of mother, one who lived, without knowing it, in unreality and so was lost to him on a personal level, and the best kind of mother, one who was full of love and generosity of spirit who had nurtured his soul. I see many things that not even my forty years as a psychotherapist had revealed.

Gradually something other than my self-condemnation and anguish arrives, I begin to understand and forgive myself. I can see clearly that I did my best with the cards I had been dealt. And so had Tim. None of this is my fault – it happened. I see in fact that we had both done magnificently.

The Ayahuasca Spirit shows me how everyone alive casts a shadow, and that of course Tim had died with unresolved conflicts. Part of my suffering when he died was that I helped Tim through this same process. It was not all guilt at what I had done, some of the remorse I felt was really his sadness and regret at the mistakes he had made, ones that, in the end, had cost him his life. After all he was certainly no saint. I see *that when Tim had come to me that first morning after his death, it was to tell me how sorry he was for more than his death. Yet I loved him enough to take his suffering into my heart and suffer it for him. Of course! He was my son; and anyway that is what love does.*

The Ayahuasca Spirit smiles and invites me into the Temple of the Goddess. I walk into the temple and am welcomed by a range of animal and plant spirits. And another journey of revelation unfolds.

The Ayahuasca Spirit revealed so many things to me it would take a whole book to share them, but most relevant here is that she took me to meet the Lords and Ladies of death, who taught me some of the secrets of death. They showed me that on death we come to eternal life through the animal body because our animal bodies take part in the mysterious and sacred renewal of life through death with total surrender. They showed me how humans have turned away from a surrender to nature in order to claim the powers of gods and, in doing so, have forgotten the wisdom of the goddesses. They told me that humanity needs to find a new balance between power and vulnerability, and the old knowledge of the goddess, which is the wisdom of the natural world, will help us. Though this will be difficult because at the heart of natural wisdom is an intimacy with death – and in modern culture we have become terrified of death.

The Ayahuasca spirit showed me that animals instinctively know the renewal of life is only through death. She revealed how they live in total commitment and surrender to life and understand death is nothing to fear because it is a natural and intrinsic aspect of life. She showed me they unconsciously recognise the true sacramental Eucharist is not a ritual in a church, it is that we eat each other to survive. Animals and plants give their lives so that others may live and instinctively know this great act of love is simply natural. They know that to continually become each other is just the way of life on Earth; we belong to each other and always have. Only the human mind thinks otherwise.

The Ayahuasca also showed me that the human mind has created a culture in which we live in fear of nature, because right at the core of natural life on this planet is death, and we try to deny death, not because we are committed to life, because we are terrified of death. We then find ourselves in a fight with nature. But a species at war with nature is at war with itself, and so we live in fear not only of others, but also of ourselves. It is another paradox: we are at war with life because we are terrified of death.

We have tried to overcome our terror of death by inventing a heavenly paradise with greener grass and bluer skies, beautiful music and serene beings of light, where everything is harmonious and there are no mosquitoes or disease, a place where somehow each of us continues to exist as a spirit, basically the same person, though with no more pain. But this would mean that death does not really exist and, as we have seen, without death life would have no meaning whatsoever. I saw that these fantastical projections of our human longing for paradise are not real; they are fantasies born out of our fear of the real truth of death. And the real meaning of death is to be found here on Earth, in life.

The Ayahuasca spirit took me to where I could see an endless stream of forms arising from the formless, on a trajectory through life that eventually took them back into the formless on death. I watched as each form and each individual life was formed in its uniqueness for a period of time before falling back into the oceanic one-ness of all life. She showed me that reincarnation is simply nature continually renewing itself through death and that this great movement of life and death is the great mystery of existence. I looked into the eyes of snakes, cows, dogs and crows, and saw in them the soul of the Earth. Animal spirits told me of their compassion for us humans. One of our dogs came and sat by me softly howling a dog-song as, one by one, different animals showed me that even though we use and abuse them, they still love and respect us. They know we know something that they do not, which means we suffer in a way they do not. And I saw other animals need us as much as we need them.

Other animals do not live in a future where tomorrow casts a dark shadow over today because all tomorrows hold the threat of death. They live in blissful ignorance that death is terrible for the individual creature because it will annihilate it. But we humans have this knowledge, and there is a terrible suffering in being the only species that knows about life and death consciously. Yet this is where the soul of humanity is born, in the crucible of our suffering. And the mysterious knowledge given to me by the Ayahuasca spirit was that the whole cosmos needs humanity to create this soul.

I was shown how in the mud of our human darkness and the struggles of our human predicament, something is cooked up that nature needs to fulfil itself. We also are nature. Our fight and alienation from nature is natural, else it would not be happening. It is our human nature to be divided against ourselves. And nature needs at least one species to divide itself against itself and give birth to the consciousness that knows itself, and therefore death. In our knowledge of death is hidden the fulfilment and meaning of nature.

The Ayahuasca spirit also took me into the temple of the goddess. She told me that this is not my home, but I will always be welcomed, because although my destiny lay in another temple, I have always honoured and respected the goddess. Surrounded by the spirits of animals and plants I was shown that not only our materialism makes us terrified of death but our traditional spirituality does also. The body is the source of life, yet most religious ideas about death give the love and life that belongs to the animal body to an artificially created idea of a 'soul', which then becomes more important than the living, breathing, flesh and blood animal body. But this reduces our beautiful animal bodies to machines and turns the living organism into a mechanism to be manipulated at will. It means we can be cruel to animals and kill them without honouring the sacrifice an animal makes when it gives its life so that we can live. In the temple of the goddess I learned that naming the beast does not give us rights over it, rather it brings responsibilities. Our intellects and brilliant minds should honour and serve the wisdom of the body, not dominate and control it.

I also saw that a god without his goddess is incomplete, yet we have banished the goddess to the wilderness of nature and the dark interior of the unconscious body. But She is the Body of Life; we cannot live without Her. Religions and their gods hold only part of the story, the rest belongs to nature and the goddess.

Life is sacred, not many of us would argue with that, but the Ayahuasca soul-medicine showed me that it is death that renders life sacred, not religious ritual or belief. The source of the soul is not a heavenly realm of light beings and angels; it is nature. The spirit must arrive in the body, not the body ascend to the spirit. Then the body will take care of our dying so that the spirit, when it is released, has true soul. But this soul is not created in a fantasy paradise that escapes the turbulence of life and love on Earth; it is forged in the struggles and surrenders of life in a mortal vulnerable body, in the almost unbearable human predicament of being a creature in conflict with oneself who also knows one day it will die.

Martin and I were in bed one night and speaking of the painful sense that at times overwhelmed us, that we were responsible for Tim's death. Tim had died 'by his own hand'. It was an accident, but maybe he had unconsciously longed for death. Maybe, under all his success and enjoyment of life, lay such a deep anguish that death was preferable to life. And, the perennial stab into my heart, maybe this was all the fault of his mother who had sometimes made her search for freedom, truth, enlightenment, love, God, whatever, more important than him because she had not understood how much he needed her.

Martin picked a book from the top of the pile of books that had now spread to his side of the bed too. It was by the Dalai Lama.

'Maybe this will give us a clue,' he said. He opened it at random. 'Some people who are intelligent and kind, attractive and strong, die young. They are Masters in disguise come to teach us about imperma-nence.' He looked at me. 'Another aspect of the truth, Anne.'

Certainly I have not thought of this before.

'I want a go.' I reached out and opened the book at random.

'It is said in our scriptures that we are to cultivate love just like that of a mother for her only child.'

My love for Tim had definitely broken my heart wide open beyond itself – but surely I don't have to love everything like this? Hoping for more guidance, I open the book and my eyes fell on:

'The Buddhist notion of non-attachment is not what people in the West assume. We say that the love a mother has for her only child is free of attachment.'

I understood completely. And I did not understand at all.

The Ayahuasca medicine explained it to me. If we have not lived and loved while alive, our spirit may be released to eternity, but it won't have much soul. The same totality of engagement that is between a mother and her only child is the engagement with life that leads to true soul. Because such a commitment to life means we are willing to engage reality totally, with no defences coming between us and our experience – and that means we suffer everything. A mother will suffer even her child's death for him or her if she could. I had no other child; I would rather have died myself than have Tim die. That is the depth of commitment and engagement with the body of life on Earth that leads us to the other side of death.

The existential anguish of knowing we will die forces us to create something that will survive our death, something that cannot die, such as love, freedom, justice, beauty, truth... forces us to create a soul so that when our spirit is released from the material world, it is more than a mere idea, it has substance and energy. It is our lives that give meaning to our deaths, not what happens after we die. We forge our souls here not anywhere else. Here on Earth, in the struggles with our human darkness, we cook up wisdom and compassion, laughter and consciousness, freedom and love. The afterlife is simply the consequence of how we have lived in this life. What matters is not what happens when we die, that will take care of itself – how we live is what truly matters.

Incarnation matters more than transcendence because the Holy Spirit lives, not in a far away heaven, but in our bodies, in everything that breathes and moves. The spirit and the body are really one. Just as the goddess and the god are not separate realities either, they are one. The spirit is the living body seen from within and the body is the outer form of the spirit.

The Ayahuasca spirit also showed me that the Body is not a map of the cosmos; it *is* the cosmos. This is the Body that lies on the other side of our ego, the other side of death. It is the Body that is the body of all of us. We are the living body of the dead just as the dead are the spirit of the living. I learned that the destiny of our species is to become the consciousness of this vast and mysterious existence of which the Body is all life and the Spirit is the dead. I was also shown that we humans with our dreadful knowledge of death, and therefore our knowledge of how precious is life, must create the love and soul that is greater than that death. And we learn this through the profound darkness in the interior of that Dark Continent – the animal body. This is because the animal body loves life enough to suffer it in its entirety, with no protection and no ego to interfere with that totality.

The very creature, therefore, whose demise is the definition of death, no heartbeat, no breath, no electrical activity in the cortex, is also the creature that is a gateway into what is beyond that death – more life. My life was never really 'mine' anyway; it was, as Kahlil Gibran wrote: 'an expression of life's longing for itself.' 'I' was the temporary guardian of an array of energies that's all.

Death is the transition from 'my' life to 'our' life because ultimately 'my' life was, is and always will be 'our' life. This is the knowledge of the goddess – that we belong to each other as much as to ourselves. There is therefore no death, only more life.

And when the Ayahuasca spirit had shown me all these things, She bowed down to me in honour of my humanity, the lonely humanity that holds the dreadful knowledge of death and, therefore, a consciousness of life that even She does not have. She then withdrew back into her wilderness temple surrounded by her writhing snakes.

13

Death Becomes Us

All religions must be tolerated… for every man must get to heaven in his own way.
Epictetus, 55–135AD

I have known the deaths of four people close to me. Their deaths were each very different. The first was the death of my old guru Osho.

I became his disciple in the 70s, a time of many experiments in living and consciousness. Yet despite my immersion in the revolutionary fervour of those times, I cannot explain how an intellectual psychologist living in a Marxist-Feminist commune in Leeds, who had never heard of enlightenment or done any meditation, listened to a tape of an Indian guru speaking on love and fear, dropped everything, went to India, fell in love with him and became his disciple. Such things are mysteries. As was my whole time with him. But then Osho was a Tantric guru.

Most people think Tantra is a kind of sexual yoga, with aromatherapy candles, deep breathing and soft lighting, but this was not the Tantra we were into. For a start being peaceful and serene had nothing to do with it.

Within many Eastern spiritual traditions there are said to be three paths to wisdom, nirvana, moksha, sainthood, enlightenment – whatever name you give to the ultimate liberation of the human spirit. The first is the 'narrow path' of discipline, simplicity and obedience, the *Hinayana* path. The second is the 'open highway' of compassionate action of service and healing, the *Mahayana* path. The third has no path. You leave all roads marked on maps to wander into the wilderness. You follow no road, not even the one less travelled. You follow only your own energy and 'dance in the fields'. This is the *Tantric* path.

High-level Bodhisattvas were supposed to have fainted when they first heard the teachings of Tantra, and gurus and spiritual teachers throughout centuries have issued dire warnings about its dangers. 'Entering Tantra is hellish.' 'Tantra is like walking along a razor's edge surrounded by the fires of hell. One slip and you are burned to a crisp.' 'The Tantric guru is in league with death.' Chogyam Trungpa the Tibetan Rinpoche, who first took Tibetan Buddhist teachings to the West, wrote in *The Lion's Roar*, 'Tantra is one of the most secret and sacred things ever heard on this Earth. It is dangerous and very powerful. Only Tantra has the power to produce enlightenment in one lifetime. It will either destroy you or enlighten you.'

Scholars have been looking for scriptures and teachings of this 'left-handed' or 'sinister' Tantra, and have never found any. Because there are none. Such teachings cannot be written down; you have to experience them.

For seven years I was a devoted disciple and gave Osho everything of myself and all that was mine. But Osho always warned us that one day we would realise there was no path, no guide, no guru and no disciple, that it had all been a very different game from the one we had imagined we were playing. And then we would fall into the void where we would discover a different kind of freedom.

That day came for me and I was enraged. I had thought Osho was a god and he revealed himself a man with all the flaws and frailties that involves. I hated him with the fury of a woman scorned and a disciple betrayed. But this also was part of the journey. If you meet the Buddha on the road, you must kill him; you must fulfil your own destiny not his.

Later I realised that of course Osho was a man; he may have been a teacher of profound wisdom and spiritual truth, but he was also human. Paradoxically I could appreciate what he had given me all the more when I realised he had struggled with some of the same challenges we all do. And with that, I made my peace with him and rediscovered him as a friend.

Then came the fate that comes to all men. A friend called me; Osho had died in the night. I wrote in my diary:

I sat down winded, hit in the solar plexus. Cars swished softly by in the road, the wisteria brushed against the window, the house creaked in the wind. In between the sounds lay a silence like an abyss. I moved to the back of the flat, into the conservatory, and looked through the garden to the trees on the Heath. I sat on a pile of cushions among the leaves and tendrils of plants. A curled, dry leaf fell to the floor. A small brown moth crawled up the window. A spider span its way between stems. From far away the phone rang repeatedly. I ignored it and for several hours was still and silent.

Suddenly I was astonished – Osho had appeared in front of me. He smiled.

'You have learned what I wanted you to,' he said.

We sat together in silence. A wind blew through the trees. Everything that needed to be communicated between us was conveyed and understood in that silence. And when all had been shared, he disappeared. He dissolved into nature, into the movements of insects, the flights of birds and the way of white clouds, into the wind, the flow of tides and the slow meanders of rivers towards seas. He dissolved into life. There was nothing left but the faint fragrance of his smile. And then that too was utterly and completely gone.

My second experience of death was when my mother died. She had a heart attack, was taken into hospital and a week later had another heart attack and died.

My mother had had a hard childhood. Her family came over from Ireland to escape rural poverty only to live in industrial poverty in Middlesbrough. Four of her siblings died before the age of five from pneumonia and her father died after an accident at the foundry where he worked. She learned there was no room for dancing or playing or having fun, to survive you had to harden yourself and follow, to the letter, the teachings of the Roman Catholic Church.

She was convinced I was headed for hell and when she died I had long before lost hope that she would ever understand me. My grief was for her sad life and the loss of what had never happened between us rather than for her death. After her death I felt no connection with her at all. Five years later, Tim's death blew open old family wounds all over again; and although I had thought I had made my peace with it all, there was more.

My Irish ancestors were landless peasants. Such people were prohibited by the penal laws of the English from obtaining an education or a profession and from owning or leasing land. A Royal Commission in 1843 reported, 'It would be impossible to adequately describe the privations which the Irish labourer and his family habitually endure. In many districts, their only food is the potato, their only beverage, water. Their cabins are seldom a protection against the weather, a bed or a blanket is a rare luxury and nearly in all their pig and a manure heap constitute their only property.' They concluded that, 'Their sufferings are greater, we believe, than the people of any other country in Europe have to sustain.'

In one of my vivid dreams after Tim died, I met these ancestors of mine, who had struggled through famines, early death and endured appalling poverty and deprivation.

Generations of my maternal ancestors are fanned out suspended in mid-air and unable to move. They are neither in hell nor heaven nor purgatory but trapped in a grey limbo with nothing to help them through their deaths into another way of being. While alive they had sacrificed everything in order to survive. Joy, happiness, love, dancing, singing, fun... these had been stamped on as frivolous and sinful and everything that was not work was punished. I saw the children of each generation had been treated with the same rigidity I had known, to teach them the harsh lesson, that unless you stamp out playfulness and fun, you will die, because every ounce of your energy is needed in the struggle to survive.

I see that my ancestors had witnessed terrible things, people with green mouths who had eaten grass to stave off starvation for a few more hours, children lying around left to die who were little more than skeletons, whole villages swept away by starvation and disease. My ancestors had managed to survive, but that is all; they had sacrificed everything that made life worth living in the process.

My mother is in the front of this generational stuck-ness. Behind her are her parents, behind them her four grandparents, back through twelve generations fanned out in suspended animation. I stare at the dreadful poverty of spirit that was the legacy of a brutal English oppression that consigned a whole people to abject misery, and I understand, at last, why my mother was so hard with me. If she had not tried to beat out of me my frivolity and silliness as she saw it, she would not have been doing her job, which was to make sure that I survived. Especially as so many of this family's children did not. Though in this dream I can see that they did not die from poverty alone, but also from the hard beatings they endured.

Suddenly Tim is here. He is a tremendous force, a being full of light and love. He stands in all his glory, full of dance, joy and laughter in front of the twelve generations of his un-dead ancestors. They had no love, joy or wisdom left in them to help them into the fulfilment of death. Tim, on the other hand, lived life to the full. He danced, played, was creative, mischievous and full of fun. He worked but only when he wanted to, and anyway he loved his writing. But in contrast to his ancestors, Tim's playing was so intense that it took him over the edge into what was dangerous for his survival until, in the end, his partying and play with drink and drugs killed him. Tim is the absolute antithesis to what came before him.

Tim kept alive the energies of dance, joy, play and creativity, but did not survive. They survived, but dance, joy and play did not. Though of course in the end, neither did they. I can see that Tim has many dimensions of being available to him in the realms of death; they have none.

I watch as Tim stands in front of them. His light penetrates their grey wasteland and begins to wake them up. These are not demons in a hell realm or people who had done evil; they are merely unable to move on. I see how they had simply done what they thought necessary in order to survive. And now one of their descendants has created enough soul while alive to wake them from their deep sleep.

They start to stir and slowly move. They begin to dimly perceive, through Tim, that when you sacrifice everything in order to survive, you end up with a life that is not worth living and a death that is not worth dying. And with that painful knowledge comes something other than their un-death.

I watch and see that their willingness to suffer the hard, almost unendurable, struggle to survive created the context for Tim and me. We would not be here but for them. And though their hardness has kept them trapped in this limbo, they have created what can now redeem them.

My mother moves slowly forward towards me. She kneels down in front of me and holds out a stone heart. She does not speak because she cannot yet, but I know she is saying sorry, she didn't know what she was doing. I weep and in the tears she can see I am at last able to forgive her for the inflexible hardness she had shown me. They are all saying it to each other now – I am so sorry, I did not know what I was doing.

Tim laughs and dances about in delight. I smile. These words should be our family motto.

Tim moves and stands next to my mother with our Irish ancestors going back through several hundred years behind him. I face them not sure what to do. They are smiling and begin to applaud. In a complete antithesis to anything I have ever received from my family before, I am being celebrated.

Tim winks. He and I have somehow managed to turn around twelve generations of our family's ignorance and fear and return it to the love that lay buried within it all along.

After this dream I began to sense my mother. It was as if she was now free to explore her life. I had conversations with her in my head in which she would say, I had it wrong didn't I? And I would say, yes you did. But, but... she would start to protest. But I wasn't having any. I would force her to admit how hard and unnecessarily cruel she had been. As long as she protested her innocence I was not going to let her off the hook.

Over the years, my conversations with her gradually evolved. She began to see how profoundly wrong she had been about me. She had thought that I was a dreadful sinner who would end up in hell, that I had no spirituality or heart. She began to see that it was not I who had been selfish, deceitful and hard, as she had told me many times; it had been her. Eventually, seven years after she had died, she was able to say sorry to me. I felt her sorrow at what she had done and she felt my understanding. And we were both released.

Tim had created much love around him and so many could be with him in his final journey into death, whether through tattoos, shamanic psychopomp, parties, poetry, music or dreams. My mother had had to do much of her journey alone because while alive she had not created much love around her. Yet in the end she managed it. My mother had enough soul that through the seven years of her death, she gradually digested the truth of her life. She had enough consciousness to suffer herself and free herself from the prison of her religion. And even though she had not managed this while alive, we found enough love lay between us to unpack the layers of fear and anger that had crushed her heart to stone. My mother is now in my life as she never was while alive.

She has become a benign presence, not deep or wise or particularly conscious, but a warm glow all the same. Maybe this is the evolution of my internalised 'mother' archetype, the one we all carry, the original template of which is our own mother. Maybe this process is, as she would have believed, her soul being cleansed in the fires of purgatory. Maybe the two of us worked across the divide of death through the unresolved energies that had come between us, and the love, buried under the weight of generations of hardship, returned. Maybe I will find her again in a new way when I die. Maybe it is more important that I am learning to love her now. Who knows? I certainly don't. Not with my intellectual mind anyway.

The third death was of my brother, Paul, who died of pancreatic cancer.

Since he died, different aspects of who he was while alive have been or are being processed by his wife, his sisters, his friends, his nieces and nephews, the young people his charity helps, his colleagues who carry on his work, his Aikido students who practise what he taught them, his many friends who loved him and so on. In a multitude of ways his life is being resolved within and between us. All those who loved him are playing their part in his journey into and through his death. And there were many who can do this with and for him because many loved him. Even some of those who had difficulty and conflict with him are part of this process because, whatever his limitations, my brother was a force to be reckoned with.

The night Paul died I had sat in meditation and felt an overwhelming sadness. I felt this sadness was not only mine it was his too. I made a promise to do all I could to help him. Two weeks later I went to my second Ayahuasca ceremony.

Darkness falls. We line up in candlelight for the first of three drinks that night. I drink and return to my mattresses and lie down. I know that my brother is in trouble and I want to help him. The Ayahuasca spirit comes to me and I tell her, 'I want to help my brother Paul.' She nods and tells me, for this journey, I must call her My Lady Ayahuasca.

We climb into a boat and begin to travel down through worlds. We keep falling through enchanted forests, the depths of the ocean, downwards in a gentle free fall until we come to land in a dark world. But it is not chilling; it is calm, peaceful and soft like velvet. I feel instantly at home. My Lady Ayahuasca tells me, 'This is the realm of

Death.'

I say, 'What about Paul. I must help Paul.'

She says, 'You know what to do.'

And suddenly I know exactly what to do.

I fly through this dark realm seeking Paul. I know I will find him because I love him, and love always finds its goal. I find my brother stuck in a narrow strip between worlds. He is half in his magnificence and glory, and half in his dark and twisted brokenness. But the two halves are stuck together and he cannot move. They are pulling in opposite directions. The glory is being drawn towards the light and God, while the unresolved darkness is a force pulling back to Earth to be reincarnated for another round of karmic completion.

I slip into the narrow layer and tell him, 'I love you, Paul.'

But he cannot hear me.

I repeat it. He hears me but does not trust me.

I tell him that I have come to take his unresolved pain into my own heart and suffer it for him because it was too much for him to process – he had had a different job to do. Our family life had been very difficult; he had tried to heal it as the only son by becoming the father our family needed, just as I as the eldest sister had tried to become its mother. I explain to him that this had been such an arduous task, he had had to pack away half of himself and, locked away in the dungeons of his unconscious, those parts had turned demonic. I show him I understand this because I'd had to do something similar.

I show him incidents in his childhood where I reached out to him with love, how I taught him to tie his shoelaces, to draw trains, to ride a bike. I show him how I had helped him as a young man and into his later years. I show him how so often I had acted from love even when he had not been able to recognise this and had judged and rejected it. I show him how although in the past I had been hurt and angry, now I understood.

One of his eyes begins to weep, and even though the other is full of rage and fury, this is the opening I have been waiting for. I begin. Piece by piece I dismantle the twisted tangle of his hatred and impotent fury *and take into my own heart his hardness, his brokenness, his impacted rage, all the fears, despairs and sadness that he had never dealt with. Tears stream down my face – but there is unspeakable beauty in this process as well as pain. This is pure energy. In life he would have judged such feelings as indulgent or irrelevant and turned away from them to get on with what he thought important, the practical demands of running the charity he had set up for dispossessed young people. He had not been able to feel all this and so I am feeling it for him.*

Eventually I have taken all Paul's unresolved pain into my heart. He is now free. He can return home to the source, to the light, to God, however we describe our final home. Paul stands up and with gratitude and love gives me the same one-fingered salute he had given me when we had said our last goodbye before he died. He flies, unencumbered now, into the Mystery, where he will be with Tim. I know they are now both at one with God, the Mystery, the vast unknowable, whatever we call it, because in their lives, they had worked to create dimensions of the spirit – and both had succeeded.

I am holding Paul's pain and anguish in my heart, feeling it in all its dreadful detail, and turn towards My Lady Ayahuasca not knowing what to do. She smiles at me. I smile back because suddenly I realise, I am Her and She is me and we are One. Our love is the spirit of life, the glorious Mystery at the heart of creation, hidden in the dark depths of the animal body with its compassion and cruelty, its instinctual anarchy and glorious being-ness. My Lady Ayahuasca and I laugh at the vast and wonderful craziness of humanity's struggles to reach the light while all the time our hearts are of darkness, our liver and kidneys too – if they come to light we die.

Later I learned that helping to release the dead in this way is called 'psychopomp'. I had never heard of it before but it is a process done by Shamans all over the world whereby they help release the spirit of someone who has died into the fulfilment of death. Though they will use not only Ayahuasca but also plants such as Peyote, Iboga, Psylocybin mushrooms, whatever grows locally. And all over the planet grow plants with medicinal properties for the soul of humanity to help us. Gaia has made sure we have all we need as we stagger through the labyrinth of being human, even right into and beyond our deaths.

The most potent death for me was, of course, Tim's.

Tim stayed with me for a year after he died. Frequently I heard his laugh and had conversations with him within me. I often felt him arrive to be with me for a while and then leave. He came to me many times in my dreams. I eventually understood that I was helping him into and through his death just as he was helping me. Then came the first anniversary of his death.

At 10.30 pm on July 31st, Martin and I sat in meditation. It was exactly one year since Tim died. I had thought so often of that night and the day that preceded it, tortured myself picturing how despite having drunk so much, Tim had staggered to Camden to find his far too potent medicine and lurched back home to smoke it. I had wondered if he had any foreboding that he had only a few more hours to live, that this was his last smile to a stranger on the Tube, the last wind through his hair, his last ever sight of the sky. I had pondered over and over whether it could have been different; was there any hint I missed, could I have done anything to save him, or had it been preordained, written in the stars, that on this day my son would breathe his last?

The permutations of possibility are infinite and I had visited nearly all of them, yet as time had gone on, I began to think less about what actually happened and more about my ongoing relationship with him. This is what matters, not that. Here is where I will find him again, not then.

Martin rang the bowl to signal the end of the meditation and stretched his legs.

'Well that was interesting,' he said. 'I got a message from Tim. I distinctly heard Tim's voice say the words, "We are connected forever."' I looked at him. 'How strange. I also heard Tim clearly tell me: "I am here, I am always here."'

We went to bed, lay on our backs and gazed into the darkness. Martin reached for my hand. 'What a year this has been,' he said. I squeezed his hand in reply. There were no words to describe either the pain or the mystery.

The next day I set off for a walk along the cliff tops from Whitehaven to St Bees.

I stare out at the horizon. The sky is dark and grey with thick clouds. The sea breaks against the rocks beneath me. I have completed the Symphony for Tim I spent this whole last year composing and listen to it on the iPhone that was Tim's last present to me. As the final track begins, I turn off the track down on to a path leading to the cliff edge. I gaze out to the horizon obscured by clouds and mist. The music takes off with organs, trumpets, horns, cellos, bells, choirs, synthesisers and dance beats. Suddenly, directly above my head, the clouds part and a bright sun shines down on me. All around me is thick dark cloud; only in a circle around me is the sun shining. I stand in this strange heavenly spotlight, turn my face up to the sun and close my eyes. As the music soars, I sense Tim in his elemental glory and magnificence. I feel his joy, his laughter and his love as his unique spirit pulses through existence. And I understand that Tim has lived his life, died his death and is now with God. He has dissolved into it all.

Under this dark sky, whose clouds have suddenly parted, I too disappear and become one with the whole of creation. I dissolve with Tim into the power and glory of the heavens, the nine choirs of angels, the communion of saints, the forgiveness of sins, the resurrection of the body and life everlasting. I have no language other than the religious imagery of my childhood to describe this ecstatic union with a mystery beyond all comprehension. Perhaps such things are best left to speak for themselves.

The final chords die away and the clouds return to obscure the sun again.

I returned home. I never thought the day would come when I would delete Tim's phone number, could not imagine I would ever voluntarily send him off into another oblivion. But I did. I picked up my phone, scrolled down to 'Tim' and 'Tim2' for the last time and deleted the numbers I have dialled hundreds and hundreds of times, that have led to thousands of words between us on the state of the world, times to meet, invitations, arguments, requests, gossip, funny stories, confessions, IT support, cries for help and so on and so on. I deleted his voice messages that I had kept for a year, hardly ever daring to listen to them because of the heartbreak in hearing his voice. I let him go once more on the next stage of his journey deep into the mystery. To where I could no longer sense, feel or stay with him.

Not long after Tim had died, a Romany gypsy had come into Martin's shop to sell him some lace. She had stared into his eyes. 'I can see you are a sensitive man,' she said, 'let me read your palm.' She held his hand in hers. 'You love your wife but she is in a lot of pain. She needs your support very much.' Martin told me that tears sprang to his eyes though he tried hard to blink them away. He did not explain that my son had died, he simply nodded. 'Her heart is broken,' the gypsy continued, 'but she will get the help she needs. There is light and love all around her.'

When Tim had been dead for a year she came again. Martin was not there but she asked for pen and paper and left him a note. The next day Martin read it. Without knowing anything about Tim's death she had written, 'The young man is with God.'

Yes he is now with God.

I no longer sense Tim's presence, he does not come to me in my dreams, and I have no more conversations with him. There is no need. The separation has dissolved and Tim is now with me always. Besides who am I to demand of anyone that they suffer the pains of existence for me? The greatest gift a parent can make is to give their child the freedom to become his or herself. Even if it is the freedom to be dead. I have let Tim go into his death, and he has dissolved beyond all form and separateness into God, the cosmos, the source, the One, whatever we call the communion beyond all duality.

Yet I know if I needed him, he would be here. And I have the strong sense there will be one more meeting between us, that somehow Tim will emerge from the formless to meet me as I die and we will be together one more time, before I too dissolve into that Mystery. How do I know this? I do not *know* it. But I feel it.

14

And Death Shall Have No Dominion

Death is only a horizon, and a horizon is nothing but the limit of our sight.
R W Raymond

Each atom in our bodies is billions of years old. Hydrogen, the most common element in the universe and a major element in our bodies, was produced in the Big Bang 13.7 billion years ago. Heavier atoms, such as carbon and oxygen, were forged in stars between 7 billion and 12 billion years ago and blasted across space when the stars exploded. This means that the components of our bodies are truly stardust. To paraphrase Genesis: 'Stardust thou art and unto stardust thou shalt return.'

Each of us is composed of the energies, forces and material of the universe. We might call this stardust, clouds of glory, cosmic consciousness, atomic elements, DNA, Spirit, yet however we describe them, these energies temporarily combine to form an entity we each call 'me'. When we die those energies are free to move and become another entity, energy, existence. Perhaps some of them even become part of another being that calls itself 'me'. But it will not be this 'me', the one I call myself. That dies. Though not all of 'me' dies.

One of the most universal myths is that when we die our exile ends and we return home to the source, God, the Dreaming, Nirvana, heaven... whatever name we use. This belief has been called the 'perennial philosophy' because it has been found in every society and culture in some form or other. It is at the heart of all the world's major religions and found in the cultures of indigenous people all over the world.

Perhaps we need such myths to ease the existential anxiety

that comes with our awful knowledge of death – that whatever we do, however we live and whoever we become, one day we will be gone. We need to believe there must be more than annihilation else what is the point of struggling so hard to survive? Or perhaps it is an attempt to ease our human alienation from our nature and instincts that we had to repress to become a member of society. No nursery would have had us if we had continued to bite strangers, steal food, kick friends and grab their toys. To become human is to lose our instinctual home in nature and maybe we hope one day to end our exile in an afterlife. Or perhaps it is simply that without an understanding that a human life has a meaning beyond itself, our struggles and death appear nothing but pointless pains with no redemptive meaning whatsoever.

Yet such myths are more than opiates for the soul; they perform a vital function. Myths and maps of what happens when we die place our human suffering in its rightful place in the cosmos and give meaning to our anguish. They help us move beyond a relentless fight for survival and the mere accumulation of power and possessions into living lives of integrity and dignity in which we create beauty out of chaos, wisdom from suffering, justice from conflict and so on. From this perspective, the primary function of myths is not to inform us of the facts of another reality or to tell us what will happen when we die; it is to enable us to live in such a way that we fulfil whatever is our destiny.

The problems arise when we confuse metaphor with fact and think that myths of death are speaking of actual realities in the same way science speaks of our material world. We then try to work out which version is the right one. We travel like a shooting star through space and encounter the deities and demons of the bardos. We dissolve into a blissful light where all is revealed. We develop an astral body and choose our next reincarnation. St Peter meets us at the pearly gates and either gives us a VIP pass or stares at the state of our soul and shakes his head. We meet ancestors and angels in a world where the grass is greener, the buildings are crystal and there are no mosquitoes. (Yes, I read this somewhere.) But if we think such descriptions of what happens when we die are describing real situations or events, we miss the point. They are symbolic descriptions and metaphors not facts.

The word 'fact' derives from the Latin *factum*, which means: 'a thing done'. Around the mid-sixteenth century it came to mean: 'something that has really occurred or is the case'. Over the centuries, this has gradually led to some confusion between 'fact' and 'truth'. They are not the same. Werner Herzog, the filmmaker, explained, making films is about truth not fact because 'fact creates norms, and truth, illumination.' Myths are truths because they illuminate our humanity, but they are not facts. This means that the question of what happens when we die has to be understood as myth not science, truth not fact, metaphor not actuality, energy not form. So with that in mind let's bring some of the ideas of this book together and explore what might happen when we die.

In death, as in life, there is sameness and difference. The sameness of our common ground allows us to meet, our differences are what make that meeting worthwhile. What, first, are the universal aspects of death?

When we die we lose all grounding. Death is the end of the life in the physical body and therefore no more breathing, eating, sleeping or running about. Death is the end of all our sensual experience, our sight, hearing, taste, smell, touch are all gone. It is the end of our intellectual minds and its capacity for language and abstract thought, the end of our defensiveness, control and ego, and the end of our alienation, tension and existential anxiety. Death is the end of our separate existence, our individual identity and the personality that we may have thought is who we are. Death is the end of literally every 'thing' and all that 'matters', the material world. Yet all this loss may not be the painful tragedy or agony that the individual self imagines. Death may not be what we fear at all.

Death involves the release of our energy from the controlling patterns of our ego, our identity, our conditioned mind and the chronic patterns of tension in the body. This control and power over our own life force is created and maintained in order that we prevent what we fear from happening. Until we deal with them, we project our fears into the future. We imagine dreadful scenarios in the future when really what we fear is what has already happened. Which is why we each fear different things. A burned child dreads fire, another is cautiously curious. Our fears from the past, such as childhood fears of being overwhelmed, annihilated, completely helpless, losing everything we love, being abandoned, left in pain and alone or whatever, are ultimately projected on to the furthest point away from us in the future – our death. Death therefore receives the projections of all of our unresolved fears. When we are dying, and there is therefore no more future to project our fears on to, there is no escape from ourselves. Then we encounter all our fears.

When we die and our ego-control dies, all the energies that our fear and control were keeping at bay arise within us full force and whatever we fear will actually unfold. This is simply because our deepest fears are of the denied energies within ourselves, which, when we die, are released from our unconscious and re-enter reality. Whether we call this process encountering demons, archetypes or hell, every single fear that had controlled us in life rears up and confronts us when we die.

The Tibetans say that even if we could not face our fear while alive, we have a period of forty-nine days grace during which we can encounter it consciously. *The Tibetan Book of the Dead* is about exactly this. Though we might say in modern language that the deities and demons of the bardos are us; the deities are the free-flowing energies that have found their fulfilment; the demons are the frightening aspects that are still unresolved. If in the dying process we contract away from the demonic energies of ourselves in more fear, then those energies will have to find some other way to resolve themselves than in the light of our own awareness, for example through reincarnation, through a longer period of suffering the truth of ourselves, in the hearts of those who love us, through our children, through a shamanic psychopomp or the prayers of family and friends.

So, in the first stage of death we lose our conscious minds and our senses. In the second we encounter our unresolved fears. In the third stage we encounter the truth of ourselves. In this stage the energy that was contained and controlled by our ego is released and who we truly are, rather than the imagined self the ego has constructed, is revealed. Our magnificence and meanness, our hatred and joy, our love and our distortions, all become apparent, because there is no controller left to hide, repress or deny our true reality. We become the pure energy of ourselves. And this energy truth-body becomes apparent to others, to the cosmos, to existence, to God and, most of all, to ourselves.

The release of our energy reveals the truth of who we are beyond our personality; as a result we discover important realities about ourselves. Or rather we do not discover anything, the very nature of the dissolution of the ego and its death uncovers them. It is revealed whether our lives are greater than our deaths or whether our deaths are greater than our lives. This is the weighing of the heart in the balance of *The Egyptian Book of the Dead*, the judgment by God of Christianity and Islam, the karmic reckoning of the Hindus, the creation of the Truth Body of the Tibetan Buddhists and so on. At this point our eternal destiny is revealed. This is the final stage of our dying.

Exactly what happens in the final stage of dying will depend upon what energies we have nurtured into life while alive and what we have neglected or denied. This process will be unique for each of us because how we have lived our lives is unique, but whatever the details, death is a profound meeting with oneself.

Death is not a singular event, it is a process that unfolds simultaneously in many dimensions and levels of reality, simply because the one who dies has many aspects. Our legacy, the gift we give to life of the energies we created, therefore also has many aspects.

Some energies of who and what we are live on in the memories of those who knew us.

Some bits of us return to Earth and the molecules reconstituted as a pebble, a beetle or the dust on the wing of a moth.

Some parts that have loved deeply may remain connected to whatever or whoever we loved until they too die.

Some parts are lost forever, have ended, are gone.

Other parts, such as our wisdom, consciousness and love, may become part of the energy fields that shape nature and reality from an overarching transcendental interconnectedness outside time and space.

Some energies may remain connected with life on Earth perhaps seeking justice or revenge, or to heal and bring peace to unresolved conflict.

Some energies may remain forever connected with our families, 'watching' over them and guiding them.

Some energies, such as our fear, greed, envy, resentment and ignorance, may return to Earth to be embodied within another ego-I in order to resolve themselves.

Some energies may return to Earth and incarnate as love and wisdom in order to bring light to the darkness that is here.

Some parts may become elements of the archetypes, memes or zeitgeist that form aspects of our human culture and psyche.

Some energies may return to the source and dissolve into the oneness, God, the light, whatever name we give the great mystery, never to emerge again.

In my experience those who love us can help us with our unresolved conflicts and turmoil even after we are dead. Maybe this happens through prayers, psychopomp or ritual. Perhaps some aspects of us go through various forms of reincarnation until we eventually create the consciousness that fulfils itself. Perhaps other aspects find their eternity through what we might call the grace of the cosmos, the vast freedom of emptiness, or the great Body of Love generated by Earth and all its creatures. Yet however we travel through life and death, and however we describe this journey, there comes in the end the final dissolution back into the source, God, the void, whatever we call that Mystery.

Here we come to rest in the is-ness, in the vast consciousness beyond duality, in the communion of saints, in the 'peace that passeth all understanding', playing harps with a heavenly host of angels, returned to the source, home with God... whatever language we use to describe the eternal resting in peace that is death. And we will each use different words to try to describe the indescribable.

I would say, we each live our own life and die our own death. The more we have given ourselves to life, in whatever way that has happened, the more profound will be our death. When we die we give all that we have created in and through our lives on Earth back to existence as we leave. This is our unique contribution to the whole, to life, to eternity, to the source from which all things flow and into which all things return. In this way we each play our part in the great mystery of existence. Together we create what created us. And on death we become it.

This is the myth of death that speaks to me. Far more important for you, however, is the myth that speaks to you. Because the myth you live by will determine your soul, and this is created in life not death. What happens after death needs concern us far less than what we do with our lives – because our lives determine our eternity. And this eternity is not after death, it is in this moment, in this person, here and now. Here is where we are creating our death.

Do we love anything enough to be willing to give our lives to it, to die for it? In which case when we die, we will live on the energies of that love. Or is nothing sacred other than our own survival in which case when we die, that's it – nothing.

Have we liberated our energy from the control and domination of our ego? In which case when we die we will become free from the pains of existence forever. Or do we still keep our energy confined within our fear? In which case it cannot disappear into freedom but will have to resolve itself in some form.

Have we created anything of significance or meaning while alive that we can give back to existence as we leave? Or do we just fight to get what we want and so have created nothing that can survive our death?

Have we created an integrity that honours life and that therefore contributes to the energy fields of existence? Or do we lack any wholeness and on death simply scatter with neither coherence nor consciousness?

Will we leave a legacy of love, truth, beauty, wisdom, justice or freedom? Or will we leave a messy set of unresolved conflicts that have to be cleaned up by our descendants or people who love us?

The answers to these questions, which are of course not questions at all but energetic dimensions of being, determine what ultimately happens when we die. Whether death is oblivion, a return to the turmoil of life or a dissolving back into the source, God, eternal peace or Nirvana, or a bit of each of these, depends completely upon how we have lived. The 'I' who asks these questions dies. Anne dies. I am a temporary phenomenon, a meeting in time and space of an array of energies who came together for a while but one day will disband. Yet this life, lived in this body, in this particular time and space, has eternal implications. Anne dies; 'anne-ness' does not.

Death is not omnipotent. There is an 'is-ness' over which death has no dominion. And love is central to the mystery of what is greater than death because when we truly love something or someone we become willing to die for them. And that makes love greater than death. Where there is love, there is no death. As St Paul wrote in his epistle to the Romans, 'here, death shall have no dominion.' And as Dylan Thomas wrote:

> And death shall have no dominion.
> Dead men naked they shall be one
> With the man in the wind and the west moon;
> When their bones are picked clean and the clean bones gone,
> Though they sink through the sea they shall rise again;
> Though lovers be lost love shall not;
> And death shall have no dominion.

15

The Kali Yuga

God is the solitude of men. There was only me: I alone decided to commit Evil; alone, I invented Good.
Jean Paul Sartre

If, on death, we become the energies of who we truly are and these energies work themselves through to some kind of resolution and eventually dissolve back into the source, what is the point of it all in the first place?

A Zen story: A fish swims in the sea. She knows nothing about seas or oceans and is blissfully unaware of the water all around her; she is simply being a fish. One day a wave washes her up on to the beach. She lies on dry sand in the heat of the sun and begins to die. She is gasping and about to breathe her last when a wave washes her back into the sea. But this time when she swims, she knows the sea in a way the other fish do not. She has become aware of the ocean and its water all around her.

All adventures end where they began, home, but though the place may be the same, the traveller is not. In the words of T S Eliot, 'The end of all our exploring will be to arrive where we started and know the place for the first time.' Or as Joni Mitchell put it: 'you don't know what you've got 'till it's gone.'

Though home is not ultimately a place. Home is here, where we all live, always, all the time. The animal body never leaves here but other aspects of us have to enter human culture and, like the fish, are ejected from this simple is-ness into time, duality and death. Yet when we die, we return to that oceanic one-ness again – and this time we know it. The great alchemical journey of life seems to involve for us humans the transmutation of pure existence into a conscious awareness of existence; and through our loss and rediscovery, the universe creates a consciousness of itself.

This conscious awareness is not thought, verbal comprehension or any kind of understanding to do with the intellectual mind; it is presence, energy, being-ness, whatever unique set of qualities a person generates through their life. Some might call this the soul, the spirit, consciousness or essence, but whatever we call it, this conscious awareness has accumulated energy and presence through the struggles and surrenders of life on Earth and remains a reality even after we have died. Though the forms in which it lives on are as varied as the living experiences that created it.

The energy of this conscious awareness will be unique for each one of us because it reflects the life that created it. Someone who struggles in athletics or sport will have a different quality in their conscious awareness from someone whose struggles were more personal within their family, which will be different again for someone whose life was dedicated to art, meditation, or saving the rainforests. The quality of our being-ness, conscious awareness or soul is connected not only with what we do, but even more with the way we do it, for example, the depth of our engagement, the degree of our commitment, our willingness to suffer with an open heart, our love, focus, determination, totality and so on. It is certainly not about doing it 'right' and making no mistakes.

A trainee monk was always in trouble. He went to his Teacher.

'What is the difference between a novice and a Master?' he asked.

'Ten thousand mistakes,' said the Teacher.

The trainee protested. 'But you've told me I am making a mistake so often I must have made at least that many!'

'No,' said the Teacher. 'You have made the same mistake ten

thousand times.'

Whatever organised religions and conventional morality tell us, the process of cooking up a soul is about something far greater than duty, doing it right or being good.

In one of the vivid dreams I find myself in a beautiful garden with fruit trees and fountains, rose bushes and water lilies in pools. Through a gap in a hedge I see Tim speaking with someone. They are laughing. I move closer. He is with our old guru, Osho. I watch as Tim is telling Osho of his great revenge on the commune and that such an insignificant little boy, who no one had paid much attention to, had written a book about the commune read by as many people as had read Osho's books. They give each other a high five and laugh because, while alive, one was a God to thousands who fell at his feet, the other was a young boy who ran around in that same adventure neglected and unimportant, yet here there is no difference between them. They see me and beckon me to join them. But I am not laughing.

Tim walks over to me, pulls my arm through his and we walk to a bench facing Osho. They are both smiling. I can see nothing to smile about because they are both dead. I turn to Tim.

'With all your gifts, you could have had a long life with happiness, children and fulfilment on Earth not just in this Garden of the Dead!'

I turn to Osho and accuse him too.

'And you could have gone off and lived in the hills enjoying the serenity and simplicity of nature in a peaceful old age.' I stare at them both. 'Well,' I demand, 'why didn't you? After all you each had a hand in your own death. It didn't have to happen. It could all have been very different.'

'Ah, but my death is not what it seems,' said Osho.

'And neither is mine,' said Tim.

They smile. I frown. They look at each other.

'Is she always like this?' asked Osho.

'Oh she'll get over it. She always gets there in the end.' Tim grins

at me. 'You know, Mum, for someone supposedly so wise, you sure are stubborn.'

I can think of a thousand replies reminding them that when they were alive they too had their share of stubbornness, but all I can manage is: 'It's all very well for you two, you're dead!'

They burst out laughing. I stand up, suddenly furious.

'My heart is broken and all you can do is laugh at me from the superior height of your serenity. What about compassion and consideration for the suffering of all sentient beings eh? You two in your lotus paradise have callously forgotten life is not a serene Garden of Eden at all – it can be hell!'

I want them to feel sorry for their appalling lack of empathy, to reach out to me with tears in their eyes for my grief, to honour with serious faces how great is my suffering that my son is dead and my life a struggle. But no. They smile. Tim reaches out and takes my hand.

'Look, Mum. When you die you will see everything in its context and the true meaning of it all will become apparent. You will see that, like us, you have completed a great journey. You have dived into both the heaven and the hell of Earth and there will be nothing left that needs to return. You will have done it all. And you will be sitting here with us laughing too.'

I cannot imagine this and tell them so.

'But you will be fine, Mum. More fine than you could ever imagine. Though for us of course, you already are.'

I look at them. They are smiling at me. I don't want to but I am smiling too.

Tim looks at Osho. 'Told you.'

'No, I told you!' Osho grinned.

'With respect, old guru, I think I told you first.'

'But you know what thought did.'

'Thought he did!'

'But did he or didn't he? That is the question.'

'Did I die or didn't I die? That's even more of a question.'

'Ha ha – a question to die for!'

They are off on their nonsensical philosophical riff bent over in laughter. I haven't a clue what they are on about but find I am laughing too. The guru, the disciple and the child, the master, the mother and the son, the teacher, the therapist and the writer, a trinity of trinities in which somehow we lost and then found ourselves. Lost and found each other too. Life, love and laughter. Death, fear and tears. We so much wanted one lot and not the other. But that's impossible. We wanted the impossible. The three of us cannot stop laughing at the joke of it all though I couldn't for the life of me explain why this is so funny. But perhaps for the death of me I can.

Their laughter is the last thing I hear as they dissolve back into this garden of heavenly delights. Yet I have to return to a different terrain – to the 'vale of tears', the 'valley of the shadows of death', where there is more to this story than just laughter. They are living in their eternity; I am still creating mine.

Like the fish, first we are in ignorant communion with existence. Then the big bang of Logos sounds and throws us into a world of duality and separation, where we come to life and start to die. Only the gods remain in the heavens where they do not die. Then out of our human community and our struggles with the mud of Earth, we evolve the singular 'I' that expands to contain the community of humanity within itself. Eventually this great 'I' expands to contain even gods and demons. But anxiety and fear arises with our creation of 'I' because as soon as I say 'I am me' and that becomes our identity, then all others become 'not-me' and dangerous; they carry the threat of harm and death.

The child psychoanalyst D W Winnicott wrote that the implications of becoming identified with oneself as a separate individual were so threatening that when this idea first arose in the consciousness of a wandering Semitic tribe in the Sinai desert it was immediately projected skywards as the great singular God 'I AM' – Yahweh. It was the only way to protect the tribe from the dreadful fact that as soon as you discover the significance of 'I', you have to face a death that is absolute and final. The awareness of 'I' only gradually returned to Earth through courageous individuals who dared to claim the uniqueness and individuality of that God for themselves. And who were willing to face death in doing so.

Through the centuries, the significance and importance of the individual 'I' entered human culture. Statues were only ever of deities until Alexander demanded one of himself because 'I am like a god.' In England in 1215 the Magna Carta brought the concept of justice to everyone, even the king became subject to the law. In the 14th century Venetian glass mirrors enabled us to see ourselves exactly as others saw us for the first time and a new level of self-awareness was born. In the 18th century the Enlightenment critically questioned age-old assumptions about freedom and rights and led to the French 'Declaration of the Rights of Man'. Then the Declaration of Independence in the United States stated: 'All men are created equal' with the inalienable right to 'life, liberty and the pursuit of happiness.' The great God 'I' had landed.

When the great singular God 'I Am' arrived, alongside a new dimension of death, he brought many freedoms, including the freedom to love whoever and whatever we choose. Love became no longer a familial duty or a political arrangement but a creative freedom that was up to us to give or withhold. In our individualised modern world we began to discover free love, and that love evolved new dimensions. Even God, who of course had similarly developed a singular identity, was forced to love us in a new way.

Depending on your point of view, God came to Earth to give us eternal life through his death, or we had to kill God to claim back the powers and glories we had projected onto him. Either way, the God dies and we claim for ourselves the powers we had once assigned to Him. The gods come to Earth, not to save us, to become us. And each time we found a god and then destroyed him or her, our humanity deepened. And when what had been projected into the heavens finally returns to Earth in its entirety then there is only one place left to go – back into a communion beyond duality once more.

Teilhard de Chardin, a French philosopher and Jesuit priest, described the universe as evolving towards a single point, where everything and its infinity of forms becomes one. He described this point as the Omega Point. This point is the ultimate Holy Communion where human beings discover their true destiny within the cosmos. Here we return home, like the fish in the sea, to discover we are what we have been seeking all along; we are the source of it all. And death takes us back here.

Our individual death takes each one of us back; our collective death will take us all back. The great secret revealed by death is that the God who created us, who became us, who we had to kill to find ourselves, this God is us. In de Chardin's words: 'We are one, after all, you and I, together we suffer, together exist and forever will recreate each other.'

Not surprisingly his ideas did not go down well with the Catholic Church; he was prevented from teaching and his books were banned. But of course, most organised religions have a vested interest in God remaining separate from us – we would not need priests otherwise. But on death one meets oneself, not an artificially created idea of a God in his heaven. Therefore as Wittgenstein warned: 'Make sure your religion is between you and God only.'

Heaven and hell, God and Satan, life and death, all are within us. They unfold within our awareness. And on death, all such duality ceases. Gods and humans, us and them, this and that, now and then, matter and spirit, death brings them all back together. And when we die, we take back into that communion all we have created during our time of separateness on Earth, for example energies such as justice, honour, integrity, truth, freedom, beauty, presence, love and the consciousness of the God we had to kill to get here. In other words, God returns home to us or we return home to God – same difference. Either way, the Creator becomes the created, the creature becomes the Creator and the circle is complete.

In this ultimate coming together, the Omega Point, the fish is back in the sea and the sea is now also in the fish. The sea of being is within us, in our awareness just as once we were in the sea of being. Alpha has become Omega and existence has become conscious of itself.

The above describes, of course, just one thread in the vast tapestry of life. There is no absolute meaning other than the ones we create, because we *are* the meaning. Each person and each culture will arrive at their own understanding of the meaning of life and death. In the East, the ultimate peak of enlightenment is the attainment of a consciousness beyond duality, where, through the death of the ego, we live in a blissful union with the source once more. Many Eastern traditions offer a variety of disciplines and teachings to help us reach this consciousness, Zazen, Vipassana, Tai Chi, martial arts, chanting, fasting, living alone in a cave, surrendering to a guru, chopping wood and carrying water... But there is another dimension beyond this enlightened consciousness. The beached fish on her return to the sea is not only, for the first time, conscious of the sea, she is ecstatic to be back. She loves the sea with every fibre of her being.

This extra dimension is significant for our modern age because our focus on the individual has meant we have moved even deeper into separation from the communion of all life. Our modern life has allowed alienations and lonelinesses to arise that were not possible in less individualised societies, where the source of one's identity is not the individual self but one's belonging to a family or particular tribe. That the belonging in modern culture is primarily to oneself not to family or community, which still carries some of the sea, makes our alienation from each other and the source even more profound. Returning to the fish analogy, it is as if the fish from the East lands in a rock pool, while the fish from the West lands on dry sand. And there is something else.

Older civilisations, closer to the earth, knew suffering was inevitable. Death was interwoven with their lives. Their children died, the crops failed, there were droughts and famines every now and then that no one could avoid. Happiness was not something to be pursued 'out there', because even if you found it for a while, you knew you would not be able to hold onto it. The only enduring peace, serenity and happiness was a quality to be found within. But our modern world is based on an assumption that enduring happiness can be found if only we pursue it hard enough. And if for some reason we are unhappy and suffering, our conclusion is that we have not worked for that happiness intelligently or diligently enough. We no longer sit with our neighbours commiserating over a cup of tea or something stronger, laughing because what else can we do in the face of what is greater than us; we frown and work even harder trying to achieve the happiness that eludes us.

No one, however protected with money and power, can escape loss. Everyone and everything we love will, one day, be lost to us; he, she or it will change, leave or die, or we will. The relentless pursuit of happiness therefore makes the inevitable losses of life and death even more difficult to embrace. Not only are we more profoundly existentially alone than ever before, it is also our 'fault' when we suffer the anguish of this inevitable loss. The belief is that if we were doing it 'right' and applying ourselves correctly, we would be happy, and so now we are ashamed when we suffer as well as suffering. We really are on the hot sand now, burning, dehydrating and gasping for breath with no water anywhere. Perhaps this is why in our modern age, which according to the Upanishads is the Kali Yuga, the dark ages, humanity's suffering is of a different order than ever before.

Many people reading this might wonder why on earth anyone would call our modern world the dark ages, especially because if you will look around you can see how well we live. We have restaurants and supermarkets with amazing food and drink from all over the world. We have films and theatres to entertain us with spectacles unimaginable to any previous age. We can travel anywhere in the world. We have homes with light and warmth available at the click of a switch. We have the world's great art and literature on our computers, all human knowledge on our smart phones. We have freedoms and rights enshrined in laws that have been fought for by generations of our ancestors. We are living the good life. Aren't we?

Yes we are. And maybe that is part of our difficulty. The more we live the 'good' life, the more we fear losing it, and death is the great reminder that over this 'good' life there is hanging something dark and threatening. What is waiting in these shadows is the end of this life – through the loss of the house and possessions that reflect our 'success', through the loss of someone we love or through our own individual death. And so the more comfortable our lives become, the more we feel threatened at the thought of its loss. As a result, alongside our individualised freedoms and great variety of happinesses there now sits a dread of the future, a fear of the unknown and an existential restlessness.

Death is no longer an inevitable accompaniment to life; it has become a constant threat to be avoided as assiduously as we pursue whatever happiness we seek. The threatening unknown other is no longer another human tribe or culture, the people who live in the land across the river, or the tribe who worship a different god from us – it has become death itself.

Whenever we meet what is different to us, what is 'other', we are presented with a choice. Crudely, we have three options. We can kill it before it kills us, put our heads in the sand and pretend it doesn't exist, or engage it with caution and curiosity. And so it is with death. Do we try to annihilate death whatever that costs? Do we pretend death does not exist? Or do we engage death with intelligent curiosity?

The first option is a fight against the reality of death. But as we all die in the end anyway, this merely staves off death a while longer. And such a fight to the death with death may end up costing us our integrity, our freedom, even our love. Then we have gained nothing yet have killed off everything that gave life its significance and meaning.

The second option is denial. Yet a denial of death ends up as a denial of life. And when we deny anything it does not just disappear, it simply continues existing outside our awareness. And then, in relation to whatever we have denied, we have no freedom, no consciousness and no love.

The third option is not an easy one either. An engagement with the reality of death involves encountering every one of our fears and suffering the full truth that death is the end of our individual life. Like Buddha said: 'If you win you lose, if you lose you lose, either way you lose.' Perhaps the art lies not in avoiding pain and loss, because that is impossible; it is in knowing which pains and losses to embrace.

Our modern culture has chosen to fight death or deny it, and has turned away from consciously engaging death and dying. As our technological might has increased, we have pushed death further away from our daily lives. We do not see the dead bodies of our relatives lying in our living rooms; we send them to hospitals where they die away from us. We would prefer not to know about the billions of animals slaughtered for our dinner and all the deaths that give us our consumer items and enable our comfort. We would rather not think about death at all. And so we deny death's existence right in the heart of our lives. And this denial has led to a grave situation.

When an aspect of our reality operates and unfolds outside our conscious awareness, it has no principled integrity to contain it; it is therefore free to wantonly indulge itself. If we think we are only kind and generous, our cruelty and greed do not disappear; they act out invisibly and all the more harmfully without our integrity to contain them. Our shadow, our repressed instinctual energies, our unconscious drives, all the aspects of our life force that we deny and pretend do not exist, come together in the unconscious realms where, unattended in that darkness, they devolve into darker and more demonic forms. Just as our conscious love creates energies and realities that we can then personify as angels and deities, our human darkness creates the energies we can personify as satanic beings and demons. Denied and consigned to the dungeons of our collective unconscious, our natural fear of death has turned into something sinister and dangerous.

Our deep denial of the power of death, whether by pretending it does not exist or creating a fantasy afterlife where we do not really die but live on in paradise, has created a great demonic force, a demon far more destructive than death. Just as we have created a God of love and consciousness with our love and consciousness, we have created a Satan of terror with our terror. This satanic force is far more terrifying than death. If one definition of a god is that he has the almighty power while his creatures hold the vulnerability, then for most species on this planet we have become a satanic God of Death.

We have the might and power to destroy them, and are doing so, while they are terribly vulnerable to us to the point of extinction. In one year over 100 million sharks are killed just for their fins, 25,000 elephants are killed for their tusks and more than 150 billion animals are slaughtered in the farming industry. Ninety per cent of the world's rhino population have been killed for their horn for Chinese medicine. An estimated 90% of honeybees have died in the US and the losses are mounting for butterflies, dragonflies and many other insects. John Scanlon, secretary general of the Convention on International Trade in Endangered Species, recently said that wildlife is under such threat that in ten years we are likely to have no more elephants, tigers, bees, lions, bears, zebras, turtles, frogs, or rhinoceros in the wild at all; a few will live in fortressed wild life parks, heavily guarded and protected from the multi-billion pound poaching industry and the trophy hunters who now use hi-tech planes and weaponry to kill whole herds from the air. With their gene pool depleted and their freedom to move restricted, even if we suddenly stopped the slaughter, their magnificence is being lost forever. We are witnessing the death of our natural world.

Naturally we humans have tried to use our powers to create lives as free from physical pain, material want and hard work as possible. In our industrialised societies, we have succeeded. What has been neglected and pushed to the edge are the consequences of this. Our lives have become more comfortable but the inevitable realities of death on this planet, where kill or be killed is the biological imperative of every living creature, have not disappeared, they have coalesced into a great collective shadow. Our human darkness is perhaps less enacted now on each other but increasingly on other species and life itself.

Richard Moss describes how we spend much of our lives trying to get what we want and hold on to it yet what we actually we need is confrontation and conflict to continue our growth and evolution as conscious beings. He has said that we need to be confronted by our own darkness else we will not discover love, freedom and wisdom, and that what is confronting humanity with its darkness now is nature. The killing fields that give us our consumer luxuries and supermarket food are out of sight and out of mind, but our unresolved issues with death have not faded, they have become a potent force that we must engage and confront.

We must face our terror of death, not only so that we can

honour nature and our interdependence with all its creatures but also because, however profoundly we try to deny the power of death, the reality is that we are not immortal gods, we are vulnerable animals. If we do not allow our natural fear of death to be part of our lives then we will continue to live in denial of the power of death and wantonly kill without knowing the destruction we are wreaking on what sustains us. This is a course that will kill us too.

It is a powerful paradox: the rise of individualism in our modern world has given us previously unimaginable rights and freedoms and created the capacity for another level of conscious love, yet it has also made us even more terrified of death and turned us into bio-terrorists. The greatest creation of human consciousness, an enlightenment of freedom and love, sits right next to another of our creations, a darkness of terror and destruction. We are approaching the Omega point of darkness as well as light.

Our collective creation of Satan has the potential to kill all life on Earth. Just as our collective creation of a God of love has the potential to save it.

The question becomes, however, not, 'Which side am I on?' as most religions imply, but 'Am I aware of both God and Satan within me?' Because, of course, the potential for both good and evil lie within each one of us. The ultimate triumph over evil is not to banish it into non-existence, which anyway is impossible, it will only devolve into more sinister forms, it is to know evil within our own hearts so completely that we are consciously free to choose again and again and again to act from love rather than fear, compassion rather than hatred, generosity rather than greed, justice rather than vengeance.

Another paradox: the death we run from because we fear it is annihilation holds the very wisdom we need to discover what does not die, qualities such as love, compassion, generosity and justice.

When we become aware of our capacity to manifest both love and harm, good and evil, God and Satan, we become free to consciously choose between them. For a start we will be able to recognise the difference. To truly discriminate between good and evil requires us to have experienced both, and to have known the potential for both within us. And for this we cannot just bite an apple; we must eat every bit of it, the skin, the pips, the flesh, and the worm that may be lurking in the core. In other words when we live life with no fear holding us back and no illusions blinding us, we will know not only the good and evil in life, we will know the good and evil in ourselves.

We will not be crippled by fear because there is nothing left to fear; we already know the worst, our own capacity for evil. And this really is the ultimate dark night of the soul, when we see the darkness in our own hearts. Once we have gone through this fire, though we will have a natural fear of death, we will not be terrified of it. We know there are far worse things than death. We have seen what is worse – our own capacity for evil through following our fear not our love.

The fear of death is more to be feared than death itself. When we do not live in fear and are no longer controlled by our fear of death, we become free to follow our love, our freedom, our energy, our desires... whatever we wish. In other words, we emerge from under the shadow of fear and start to live. The more we come alive, the less we fear death, because death is part of life. The less we fear death the more we become able to truly love, because true love entails being willing to die for what we love. And when we are no longer afraid of death, we will be free to love and we will love our freedom. The greatest good is not eternal life; it is to live one's life and die one's death in love and freedom. What greater good can there be than this?

16

Loss and Liberation

The price of freedom is death.
Malcolm X

Tim's death was the most profound event of my life. It left no area of my life untouched and involved every aspect of my work, my relationships and myself. Everything changed. Overnight, so many things that used to matter ceased to be of any importance to me whatsoever. From being someone who enjoyed her work, meals out, shopping, success, a tidy house, new clothes, gossiping with others, who cared what others thought of me, who thought she was pretty much together and in charge of her life, who was full of dreams for the future in which there would be family holidays and grandchildren, I became someone I no longer recognised. I walked for hours along cliff tops and in the fells, and left my phone at home. I preferred to sit by the fire and knit than go out for dinner with friends. For weeks I would meet no one and hardly speak. From being someone who generously gave to others and nurtured friendships, I became someone who needed others and had time only for those who reached out to me. When Tim died, the old me also died.

Many people said, perhaps trying to ease the dreadful pain of my loss – 'You'll get over it in time, Anne.' But you do not come back from the dead; I won't ever get over the loss of Tim. What's more I don't want to. But grief is a complex journey through some strange terrain, and certainly the dark days of staring for hours at a blank wall of inconsolable loss have gone. As have the days of remorse and guilt that somehow his death was my fault. But no one goes through a death unscathed, and when someone you love dies, you are transformed at root.

Four months after Tim died, Martin and I went to grief counselling. Tim's death had crashed into us as absolutely as a tsunami smashes into a house of straw and the centre had not held, we were falling apart. I wept, read 'spiritual' books and wanted to die; Martin raged, worked to support us and had lost me as well as Tim. Our different griefs stared at each other across the chasm that had cracked into existence between us. Statistics have shown that only one in five marriages, where one is a stepparent, survives the death of a child; I can understand why. When Martin and I tried to talk about what was happening, my tears made him angry and his rages made me weep. I was living in the half-light of the spirit world with the dead; Martin was working to keep our life together. I was a parent and Tim's mother; Martin had no children and was Tim's stepfather. I didn't want to live; Martin was struggling to keep us alive.

The counsellors were lovely people, kind and caring, and the counselling was helpful for Martin. It did nothing for me. All I could manage was to weep and say: 'Tim was a lovely person, I loved him so much.' One time I tried to share how lonely I felt in my grief because none of my friends and not even Martin under-stood. The non-parents did not understand the depth of loss and the parents did not want to even imagine such a loss. How could it be otherwise? The counsellors did not understand either; they likened Tim's death to losing a parent. But a child dying is like no other loss.

I found a degree of solace with other mothers who had lost children. We tried to share our loss describing it as 'the worst pain imaginable', 'unspeakable agony', 'utter devastation', 'worse than my own death'. But we knew that only other mothers in our situation understood the depths of what could not be spoken. Many mothers I spoke with had also, like me, been overcome by a dreadful remorse that compounded our grief, a guilt that cut into us like knives that somehow our child's death was our fault.

Why is the death of one's child so uniquely terrible? Did we want to die because the maternal bond is even stronger than the desire to live? And is that because the connection between a mother and her child is so instinctually visceral and intense, more potent than any separate individuality? And why did so many mothers I spoke with feel responsible for the deaths, as well as the lives, of their children?

When Tim finished his degree in psychology, he began to write. He rented a room in a house shared with other aspiring artists, writers, musicians. There was one heater for the whole house. Which room it heated depended on who had partied least the night before and was up first. Peeling lino covered broken floorboards. Each window had curtains of mismatching colours and different lengths. They got by on whatever jobs they could find until they hit it big, which they seemed pretty certain they would one day. Their fridge may have been empty, but their heads were full of dreams.

Between organising music events and part-time work in bars, Tim wrote. He was going to write the story of his childhood he told me. 'But whenever I write, I feel that you are looking over my shoulder. It's hard to get into it with you there reading everything I write.'

Becoming an individual is a far more complex operation than a cut through an umbilical chord.

'Tim, you must order me to go away and leave you alone,' I told him. 'And if I don't, then you must stab me with your pen or something – anything, but you have to get rid of me.'

Maybe this is why Tim wrote a book that told only half the story. In order to become himself, he had to pull out what was even mightier than the sword to slay the mother that was in his way. It is not only the Buddha we must kill if we meet him, we must 'kill' the Mother too. She was after all our first guru, the one we once loved without reservation.

Children are a part of the mother. They come to life within her. Our mother's body is our first home. She is for a while our whole universe. Our mother was once the omnipotent, omnipresent being who was our whole world, yet, just as completely, she was profoundly and devastatingly human. And even if later, in an attempt to escape the threat of her psychic intrusions upon our vulnerable individual psyche, we project this overwhelming power skywards as a male God, we cannot escape. The mother is a constant reminder that each of us is not only a distinct and unique self but also an interdependent inter-connection with what is greater than us. And until we expel her from our psyche, our mother's very existence constantly presents a threat to our separate individuality. It is no accident that the most individualised cultures have a male God and have banished the Goddess to a far away wilderness.

Mothers have a dreadful power. For a while she holds absolute power over us, and we all know what absolute power tends to do. Freud said the dark secret that binds society together is the hidden wish in all men to kill the father. Perhaps a deeper secret is the wish in every individual to annihilate the mother. Maybe our sentimental expressions of love in flowers and cards on Mother's Day are attempts to hide the guilty collective secret that, however much we may love her, we would also like to be free of her.

Yet in the heart of that power there lies as dreadful a vulner-ability. 'In pain shalt thou give birth' refers to more than the contractions of labour. We give our children the freedom to become separate from us, to become themselves, and if we do our mother's job well we will even hand them the sword with which to kill us. But though our children must become free of us, we are never free of them. Perhaps that is why the death of a child is so potent – it is our death too. Yet even death does not end the responsibilities of motherhood.

I am the mother of a dead son. I had to look right into the face of Tim's death and let it speak to me of things I would rather not know. And because I am his mother, I would leave no stone unturned until I found him again – however painful the revelations of that journey. The only way to develop eyes that can see into the dark night of death is to gaze into your own darkness. Which means, if I were to find Tim again, I had to see into the darkness within myself.

Death dismantles the ego. My ego has not been constellated around power, status or wealth but around being loving, caring and wise. I was desperately seeking the love and wisdom my childhood had lacked so profoundly, and I did this by trying to become the source of that love and wisdom rather than becoming and being myself. I sacrificed myself on my own altar. As a result when I encountered death through Tim's death, and my ego was dismantled too, I had to see where I had *not* been loving, caring and wise. I had to let every mistake I made as a mother accuse me all over again. I had to see my failings written large and let them break my heart with regret. And I had to see that though I may have been a 'good' mother in some arenas, I was a 'bad' mother in others.

In the first part of Tim's life he had loved me unconditionally with the openhearted totality of a child. I was often absent. Not because I did not love him, but because I was absent from myself. I found myself and turned around to meet him, only to find aspects of him had wandered off and were absent from me. When he was there, I was gone; and when I was there, he was gone.

When I realised how deeply our time in the Rajneesh commune had deprived Tim of the family life he needed, I was determined to bring him in from the cold and heal our family. For two years we held family meetings every Thursday, and we all had to agree before this arrangement could be changed. Tim had been born into a nomadic unsettled existence with an insecure mother on a pilgrimage to find herself; I hoped that just as every dream has in it the seeds of its own failure, so every failure has in it the seeds of its own redemption. I hoped we could go on another journey, together this time, one that would show Tim the very search that had taken me away from him, had given me myself and now I could be with him in the way he needed. I had fondly imagined Martin and I would show Tim how much we cared and all would be fine. That was the hope anyway. The first meeting revealed the reality.

Rather than sit side by side on the sofa presenting what might look like a united front 'against' Tim, I had sat on the sofa, Martin on a chair. I had hoped Tim would sit next to me, but he took another chair and sat in the corner, arms folded, his baseball cap pulled over his face.

I began. 'I want to deal with everything that has happened between us because I want to make our family work and I am absolutely committed to this. I know I have made mistakes, and I regret some of what I have done, but I am determined to redeem it all as best as I can. I want us to be a loving family again and I'm ready to do whatever is needed for this.'

Tim shifted in his chair, his expression unforgiving and resentful.

Martin leaned forward, placed his elbows on his knees, his chin in his hands.

'I am absolutely here too and, like your mum, I am willing to go with the process of these meetings wherever it takes us.' He looked at Tim who stared at the wall. 'I have not taken care of you, Tim, as I now know I should have done. And I am very sorry about that and I want to put it right.'

I had assumed in these meetings we would show Tim how much we cared and, when we talked openly, Tim would do the same, but he maintained a tight-lipped silence in the corner with his baseball cap pulled down over his eyes. I tried to persuade him to talk with us, but the more I tried to motivate, convince, cajole, influence or tempt him, the more contemptuous his scornful looks became. There seemed no way through this; however much I loved and cared for him, my mistakes had been too great, too many and this was too late. I bent over and put my head in my hands. I had messed up the most important thing in my life. I had failed as a mother and my son was lost to me. Suddenly I heard myself cry out – 'I wish I'd had a mother like me!' And I sobbed.

I felt a hand on my arm.

'Here you are, Mum.'

Tim had moved from the corner to give me a tissue from the box I had earlier made sure was in the room. I had thought they were for him, had never imagined I would use them first. Tim put his arm around my shoulder as I wept.

We had begun, though not at all as I had planned.

Tim, Martin and I met every Thursday for two years. We went back into our painful and turbulent past, shared our memories and feelings, acted out old dramas in new ways. We struggled, shouted, wept and laughed. We explained, listened, shared what we did not know could be spoken. We told our dreams, our hopes and our fears. We unearthed what had been lost within and between us and gave ourselves to each other all over again. Each meeting ended with one or other of us weeping in the middle of the other two, or with us falling about laughing. In the tears and laughter, we found each other all over again. We not only redis-covered each other, we found that family love has the power to heal many other wounds, ancestral pain from generations of struggle as well.

I had written about our family meetings and told the Zen story of a seeker who visited a wise monk and asked for the secret of a happy life. The monk told her, 'First the grandparent dies, then the parent dies and then the child dies.' The seeker was outraged. 'What are you talking about? That is not happiness, that's unhappiness!' 'Ah, you are wrong,' said the Master. 'Unhappiness is, first the child dies, then the parent dies, then the grandparent dies.'

Tim would say that these meetings gave him the context and language to write as he did, and without them he would not have been able to develop his understandings and insight. I would say our family was learning the right order of suffering, and in doing so we were healing the wounds of history. However we described it, we had released our family love and found each other again.

Then Tim died and his death ripped those wounds open all over again.

How would I describe our family when I stared into the even more profound absence of death? Would we find each other this time? Our love had reached across time and healed the past, but would it manage to bridge the great divide of death? I desperately needed it to. I needed it to find Tim again. And I needed it for myself. Because only a love that transcends death offers redemption for a mother whose son has killed himself, because that is what Tim did, however unintentionally.

Tim got himself to Camden and back home with his opium to roll into cigarettes and smoke. He was so drunk he didn't know what he was doing, yet he was able to construct those deadly roll-ups, the ends of which he drunkenly threw out the window where we later found them beneath his bedroom window. He was extremely intelligent, but not enough to realise that his tolerance had disappeared and his body was no longer able to travel with him into the crazy delights of his abandoned let-go. He loved his wife, his life, me, but not enough to stay here. Was his inner pain so great that death became a friend? Did he want to die? Did Tim take drugs to embrace life, or to escape it?

Sweet sentimental descriptions of a mother's affection will get me nowhere. The only redemption possible for a mother, whose son has died by his own hand, is in a love that has seen into our human darkness and survived it. And this love is not the pearl of great price created in the gritty irritation of life; this is the diamond, forged two hundred kilometres under the surface of the Earth at a temperature of 800C in a pressure 50,000 times atmospheric pressure – the hardest of all loves, and indestructible. This is the only love that can redeem a mother like me.

Perhaps we all need the redemptive power of such a love; after all, it is the complexity of a mother's love that makes us human. The uncomplicated loves of grandparents, dogs, gurus and therapists might be balm for our inner wounds but this love is not the love that forces us into our humanity. That power belongs to a love with a mother who was once our whole world, and who we loved with the absolute totality of innocence, and then had to leave to find ourselves. We each have had to turn away from this paradisiacal one-ness to become separate, unique, a person in our own right. And it is the mother who throws us out of this paradise.

Her imperfect love ensures we leave the Garden of Eden of communion with all life for the jungle of culture and society, where we discover loneliness and death. The source of our humanity is not unconditional love with empathic understanding and unceasing positive regard; it is a much tougher love that has struggled with being and non-being, existence and annihilation, war and peace. And this love is in the long marriages in which we suffer each other's darkness to the end, and it is in the psychobiology of the love between a mother and her child. This is the kind of love that renders us human, in which we do our worst to each other and still there is love.

Two weeks before Tim died I had a dream.

A baby lies in a large Moses basket decorated in gold and jewels. The baby is a prince. The swaddling clothes are furs and rich fabrics, but they are too tight. I can see the baby is struggling to move and going red with the heat. I feel I should not interfere, however, because I am just an ordinary person and this baby is a prince. Yet no one seems to notice the baby's distress. I decide that whether I get into trouble or not, I will help this baby. I loosen the swaddling so that air can flow through and cool him. And with looser binds he is able move his limbs more freely. As I do this, the baby opens his eyes. To my complete surprise it is Tim. He looks me straight in the eye. 'I knew you would know what I needed,' he says.

I told Tim the dream. He asked what I thought it meant. I suggested,

'Maybe in your life now you are enjoying the security and holding that being in Jo's family gives you, where you are cosseted like a little prince. (He was very much loved there by them all.) But I, who did not hold you with enough security and swaddling when you were young, understand more about our needs for freedom.'

He had pushed back his flat cap, scratched his head and said,

'Mmm… I'll get back to you on that.'

He never did. Two weeks later he was dead.

I was the best of mothers and the worst of mothers.

As are perhaps all mothers.

After Tim's death, Martin suggested that perhaps it had been a prophetic dream in which I helped loosen Tim's attachment to the body to ease his passage into death. Who knows? Maybe it was.

In my search into the meaning of death I was looking for Tim, I was looking for myself, I was looking for understandings that would redeem my aching sorrow about my less than perfect mothering and I was looking into death. But in the early days of Tim's death, I was too lost in my grief to gaze into the murky depths of our collective unconsciousness and the psycho-politics of our culture's denial of the power of the mother. Besides, I was struggling with the vulnerability of the mother not her power, a vulnerability to a love that will let her child kill her if he or she needs to. Which is why the death of an only child is worse for the mother than her own death would be. But in that loss is a different kind of liberation.

I will never look into Tim's eyes ever again, and he will never again look into mine; his eyes are gone forever, just as, one day, so will mine. But although the living, breathing reality of Tim has gone from life forever, which is the inconsolable, irreplaceable and irretrievable reality of death, the love that those eyes communicated is not gone. It is here. It is always here. Yet it was created between two flawed human beings. Love is created in our mortal vulnerabilities not our perfections, in the challenges of our human predicament not in an unassailable serenity beyond it all. Love is made in the meeting of separate bodies who die.

All love that transcends death is created in the bodies of human beings who will one day die. Which means that even the eternal depends upon death for its creation. Life in a body is founded on a multitude of deaths – the deaths of our ancestors who had to kill to survive, until they died, and the deaths that provide us with food every day. The love that transcends this law of life, that for one thing to live another has to die, is also created through living life in a body; and that life depends upon death. So even the liberation of love that allows us to triumph over the losses of death depends upon death. Death is the dark heart of not only life on this planet, but also eternity.

We can turn away from the awful power of death as much as we like, and create visions of life in which there is no darkness, no fear, no existential anxiety and no dark shadow of death hanging over every moment. In fact many of us are desperately trying to do just that with our various dreams, hopes and visions of a future with no hatred, no destruction and no war. I certainly was, until Tim's death taught me differently – that light without darkness, peace without war, love without fear, compassion without suffering, and life without death are absolutely impossible.

I was always seeking the bliss of somehow being beyond the turmoil and anguish of my life. I had not realised that through denying the power of death to completely break our hearts, we lessen our connection with life. Yet Tim's death taught me to embrace the losses of death, because that is the only way to discover the release of love that death also engenders. And however much we may try to turn away from the heartbreak of death, in the end none of us escapes. Everyone and everything we have ever loved will one day change, leave or die, or we will.

In one of the last vivid dreams I meet up with Tim and he takes me into the Spirit world. We move through a crowd of spirits on our way to another realm. These spirit beings part to let us through, and as we walk between them, they bow down to us. Not just nods of the head, deep bows from the waist. Some even prostrate themselves. Tim is taking it in his stride but I tell them to stop, this bowing stuff is irrelevant – what matters is our interconnection not our ranking on some phoney hierarchy.

Tim laughs at me. 'But, Mum, if they want to bow why not? Besides you come on more superior telling them where it's at in your liberal equality number than you are when they are bowing to you!'

The people-spirits around us smile and begin to bow again. I am surprised that this time I accept it as completely natural, as if I were an empress. Suddenly I remember a well-known psychic, Rhea Powers, told me many years ago I had been an empress in Ancient China. I would order people to be beheaded on a whim, raise my little finger and whole villages would be put to death. She told me this lifetime was about making reparation for such abuse of power. I ignored it. It sounded to me like one of those reincarnation delusions of grandeur, and anyway I have never felt remotely like an empress. But she had been very insistent. Though strangely I do have Chinese antique furniture, Chinese robes, and while Hollywood thrillers leave me confused, I can understand the subtleties of Chinese movies without knowing how or why.

In this dream I am the Empress who has divine right to supreme power – but no personal freedom, the role of Empress is all. I see in my current life I have no status or privileged position, but enormous personal freedom, the reality of myself is all. These polar opposite positions, each with their different vulnerabilities and powers, seem to come together in me in this dream. I see that whether I describe it as the karma of past lives, destiny written in the stars or the socio-biological unfolding of a particular combination of genes and circumstance, this lifetime has been for me about transcending both these polarities. And there is only love that can bridge such a great divide. My life has been about learning to love.

But I also see in this dream, learning to love is not easy. There is only one way to open our hearts beyond themselves – our hearts have to be broken open again and again. I have certainly loved and lost many times. And in this dream, in the middle of the deepest heartbreak of them all, the death of my only son, there is no longer anywhere to hide from the truth of love.

Animal spirits are joining us now. I see the Jaguar Spirit, with her dark wisdom of the jungle. I see the Wolf Spirit with the ice blue knowledge of hell in his eyes. I see the Snake Spirit with her forked tongue that can tell both truth and lies because she knows that only poisons have the power to be medicines. I see the Elephant embody the memories of history, the Bee, that we belong to the matrix as much as to ourselves, and the Shark, with her cold understanding that in life on Earth you either kill or are killed. And I see the destiny of humanity is to embody the truth of love. Because we know the terror and alienation that is love's opposite, we therefore know love in a way no other creature can. The human heart is the heart of the cosmos.

With my dead son by my side, I see the human heart has to open beyond itself, open to the whole of existence. Broken open until every creature can find a home in what was once a fortress built against the ultimate heartbreak of death. And in the middle of my heartbreak at Tim's death I see I have to let my own love break my heart. Tim's death has broken me open to love.

I am bowing too now. We are all bowing. I can see now that these other spirits, both animal and human, had known all along: they were not bowing to me, they were bowing to love. We are all bowing, not to each other, to love. To a love that will break open our hearts ruthlessly and repeatedly until, in its ruins, the whole of existence can find a home. And death is an intrinsic and essential aspect of that great journey into love.

'Now you see,' says Tim.

17

Messages from a Black Hole

If you would indeed behold the spirit of death, open your heart wide unto the body of life. For life and death are one, even as the river and the sea are one.
Kahlil Gibran

Tim has been dead four years. It is a beautiful summer and in our market garden the birds sing, the bees make honey, the hens lay eggs, and our fruit and vegetables grow in abundance. Tim is with me, in me and around me as I too return to life, but to a life that includes death. Though I still have days when I weep. And I still do not 'know' what is death. But I now know what I did not know before, that death has to be here as much as life.

What is death?

Doctor: Death is the end of electrical activity in the neo-cortex.

Philosopher: Death does not exist for the living, only for the dead.

Hindu: Death does not exist, it is part of the illusion of maya.

Buddhist: Death is a return to the freedom of emptiness.

Taoist: Last night I dreamed I was dead, how do I know today I am not dead and dreaming I am alive?

Tantrika: Death is not a problem to be solved but a mystery to be lived.

Jew: Death is part of life – Oy vey.

Christian: The good news is that love is greater than death.

Sufi: Death is not an event in the future, it happens every moment.

Linguistic Philosopher: The question 'what is death?' is

meaningless because it uses language designed for one form of enquiry in a domain that uses language differently.

Poet: Death is the dark inevitability in every blade of grass!

Biologist: Death is the engine of evolution; without it we would not be here.

Psychotherapist: We project our fear of the unknown on to death; therefore to know death we must know ourselves.

New Age Guru: We create our own reality and so death is whatever we make it.

Agnostic: Death is, and always will be, a mystery.

Neo-Atheist: We are born, live and die – end of story.

Existentialist: The answer to 'what is death?' is to be found *in* life not after it.

Shaman: Put this in your pipe and smoke it – all will be revealed.

Someone recently bereaved: Death is inconsolable loss.

I cannot say with any certainty what is death, but I have at least understood that life and death are inextricably linked, each needing the other to give it existence and meaning. A life without death is not life; just as a death without life is not even a death, it is nothing. And I now honour death because I have learned:

- Without death, life would have no meaning.
- Life continually renews itself through death.
- Death is the engine of evolution of life on this planet.
- Death rescues life from being endlessly banal, repetitive and insignificant. Death brings significance to every situation, every event and every moment. If we lived forever we would end up identical clones; everything would eventually happen to each of us on an infinite loop – forever.
- Without death we would be singular, inviolate and no longer human. Without death it would all be about power

not vulnerability, self not mutuality. Our survival strategies seek the powers of the gods, but death ensures we remain in touch with our humanity.

- Without our mortal vulnerability we would not need each other. Death is at the root of all mutual co-operation, collective action and interrelationship.
- The existential challenge of our human predicament, which is the knowledge of one's own death, impels us to create that which does not die. The awful finality of death is the fuel of creativity.
- Without death there would be no becoming, just a sameness that permeated it all.
- Death impels us to conceive of the future, a possibility in which we, or something we have created, survives death. Death creates time, which creates vision, which creates creativity, hope and potentiality.
- The reality of death gives the living body that will die, whether that body is ours, the body of another person or the body of another creature, value and significance. Because we know that, one day, the life of that body will be no more, the body becomes precious.
- Without death nothing would be sacred. A celestial projection of perfection, a heaven with angels and saints or a white light in which all is perfect bliss, does not render life sacred – death does.
- Without the preciousness of life created by the reality of death there would be no love and no need for love. Only life in a vulnerable body that dies can make love. Death ensures that although love may not be all we need, we all need love – and therefore must make it while we can.
- Our knowledge of death makes being alive a sacred imperative to create what is eternal – love, truth, beauty, wisdom, justice, consciousness or whatever is our calling. In other words, the inevitability of death forces us to create a soul.

And if we do not create these things while alive, we cannot create them when we are dead.

- Death creates in us the capacity for compassion. Knowing not only that one day we will be dead, but also that each and every one of us will die, inspires us beyond the instinctual anarchy of a fight for survival into a compassion for all sentient beings. Because we know they will die even if they do not.

- Other animals are alive but do not *know* they are alive; they do not therefore know death. Only we humans have separated ourselves from the communion of life where all is one, and therefore hold the knowledge of individual death. Humanity and death are inextricably linked. Only a creature divided from itself and life can look back at itself and know itself. And only such a creature divided from the holy communion of all life can know death.

- Our experience and knowledge of death create our longing for transcendence. Our mortality creates the sacred. The source of spirituality and religion is not the abstract idea of a spirit, it is the vulnerability of the animal body that dies.

- Death only exists for the individual body. Death does not exist for the body of all life. Death is simply the transformation of one form of life into another.

- Death reminds us that life on this planet, with its north and south pole, its in and out, dark and light, self and other, hot and cold, male and female, chaos and order, life and death, always holds a hidden opposite without which the homeostatic balance that maintains life, and even existence itself, would be lost.

- Until we know the suffering that longs for death, we have not come fully alive, we have stayed on the surface. Life, like death, includes everything from the brightest light of wisdom and love to the darkest night of ignorance and fear. And the consciousness of humanity has to know both to fulfil its destiny as the consciousness of the cosmos.

- Ideas of finding happiness and serenity away from the inevitable suffering of death are the superficial desires of a spiritual materialism. We have to find happiness and serenity *in* the inevitable suffering of death. And that is a very different journey from seeking happiness by getting what we want.

- There is only one God greater than the God of death, the God of love. And that God is us. We make the love that has brought this whole world into existence.

- At the level of the body, our sexuality makes the love that gives birth to the whole of humanity, which then creates the world around us, externally in the form of society and culture, internally in the creations of the human mind that has constructed this world of form from the energy flow that is life.

- At the level of consciousness, through living life, we create a consciousness of life that transcends death. It transcends death because, when we die, life does not die, and that consciousness belongs to life, not the individual. The individual is the means, not the end.

- At the level of love, we are the love that transcends death and brings light to the darkness, the love that heals the pains of existence, redeems the ignorance of matter and brings the whole of the cosmos home to itself – to love. Which was the reason for existence coming into being in the first place – to find itself.

- Death ensures we make life into more than a mere struggle for survival, which anyway is futile as, whatever we do, each and every one of us dies.

- Without the dark shadow of death hanging over every moment, there would be no light of wisdom and no redemption through love. Light and dark, love and fear, life and death, we cannot have one without the other.

- Death makes life so precious, our love makes us willing to die so that others might live. Which is why love is greater than death.
- Love, Life and Death form the holy trinity that spins reality into existence. And these three are one. And this three that is one is the all that is us.
- Love renders our lives greater than our deaths.
- We project our hopes on to love and our fears on to death; neither are what we hope or fear. Both love and death are far greater and more mysterious.

18

Who Dies?

Are you the one who comes to me and is with me in my dreams?
Or are you the one who's completely gone, is absent and unseen?
Do you dance among the stars in a realm beyond us all?
Or is this a free fall into loss and you've ceased to exist at all?
Are you the one who lives on?
Or are you the one who died?

Are your eyes on a far horizon under a different sun?
Or are you blind and frozen and in all directions gone?
Will we ever meet again in joy and eternal light?
Or is there no relief for my grief and all is perpetual night?
Are you the one who lives on?
Or are you the one who died?

Do we arrive trailing clouds of glory into Earth's dirt and hurt?
Or do we fight through a thousand lives of birth, death and rebirth?
Do you live?
Or have you died?

Or are you both the one who lives on and also the one who died?
And is that why my heart is broken in two and half has died and
*   gone with you?*
And we are both the ones who live on,
And we are both the ones who died.

Thank you to everyone who helped me through the deepest journey of my life. I am eternally grateful. And thank you, Tim, for being you.

www.dimensionsofdeath.net

Of the many books that grew in a pile by my bed, these are the ones I found particularly helpful:

God in All Worlds Ed. Lucinda Vardey (Pantheon 1995)
Knowing Yourself Barry Long (Barry Long Foundation 1983)
My Way, The Way of the White Clouds Osho (Element 1995)
A New Science of Life Rupert Sheldrake (2005)
On Life After Death Elisabeth Kübler-Ross (Celestial Arts 1991)
Staring at the Sun Irvin Yalom (Piatkus 2011)
Staying Connected Rudolph Steiner (Steiner Books 1999)
The Art of Dying Peter and Elizabeth Fenwick (Continuum 2008)
The Book of Job Stephen Mitchell (North Point Press 1987)
The Future of Man Teilhard de Chardin (Collins 1969)
The Myth of Freedom Chogyam Trungpa (Shambhala 1988)
The Tibetan Book of Living and Dying Sogyal Rinpoche (Rider Reprint 1996)

Nirvana helped me more than I have been able to describe in this book. She can be reached for psychic readings at:
sandrahailes@gmail.com

Other Books by Anne Geraghty
In the Dark and Still Moving
How to Make Your Relationship Work

www.dimensionsofdeath.net

BOOKS

O is a symbol of the world, of oneness and unity. In different cultures it also means the "eye," symbolizing knowledge and insight. We aim to publish books that are accessible, constructive and that challenge accepted opinion, both that of academia and the "moral majority."

Our books are available in all good English language bookstores worldwide. If you don't see the book on the shelves ask the bookstore to order it for you, quoting the ISBN number and title. Alternatively you can order online (all major online retail sites carry our titles) or contact the distributor in the relevant country, listed on the copyright page.

See our website www.o-books.com for a full list of over 500 titles, growing by 100 a year.

And tune in to myspiritradio.com for our book review radio show, hosted by June-Elleni Laine, where you can listen to the authors discussing their books.

MySpiritRadio